Afrikakorps

By the Editors of Time-Life Books

Alexandria, Virginia

Time-Life Books Inc.
is a wholly owned subsidiary of

The Time Inc. Book Company

President and Chief Executive Officer:
Kelso F. Sutton
President, Time Inc. Books Direct:
Christopher T. Linen

Time-Life Books Inc.

EDITOR: George Constable
Executive Editor: Ellen Phillips
Director of Design: Louis Klein
Director of Editorial Resources: Phyllis K. Wise
Director of Photography and Research:
John Conrad Weiser

PRESIDENT: John M. Fahey, Jr.
Senior Vice Presidents: Robert M. DeSena, Paul R.
Stewart, Curtis G. Viebranz, Joseph J. Ward
Vice Presidents: Stephen L. Bair, Bonita L.
Boezeman, Mary P. Donohoe, Stephen L.
Goldstein, Juanita T. James, Andrew P. Kaplan,
Trevor Lunn, Susan J. Maruyama, Robert H.
Smith
New Product Development: Yuri Okuda, Donia
Ann Steele
Supervisor of Quality Control: James King

PUBLISHER: Joseph J. Ward

The Third Reich

SERIES DIRECTOR: Thomas H. Flaherty
Series Administrator: Jane Edwin
Editorial Staff for *Afrikakorps:*
Designer: Raymond Ripper
Picture Editor: Jane A. Martin
Text Editors: Stephen G. Hyslop, John Newton,
Henry Woodhead
Researcher: Robin Currie
Assistant Designer: Lorraine D. Rivard
Copy Coordinator: Charles J. Hagner
Picture Coordinator: Ruth Moss
Editorial Assistant: Jayne A. L. Dover

Special Contributors: Ronald H. Bailey,
Timothy Foote, Lydia Preston Hicks, Donald Dale
Jackson, Thomas A. Lewis, Brian C. Pohanka,
David S. Thomson (text); Martha Lee Beckington,
Maggie Debelius, Oobie Gleysteen, Helga R. Kohl,
Marilyn Murphy Terrell (research); Michael
Kalen Smith (index)

Editorial Operations
Copy Chief: Diane Ullius
Production: Celia Beattie
Library: Louise D. Forstall

Computer Composition: Gordon E. Buck
(Manager), Deborah G. Tait, Monika D. Thayer,
Janet Barnes Syring, Lillian Daniels

Correspondents: Elisabeth Kraemer-Singh
(Bonn), Christina Lieberman (New York), Maria
Vincenza Aloisi (Paris), Ann Natanson (Rome).
Valuable assistance was also provided by:
Elizabeth Brown (New York), Christine Hinze
(London), Nihal Tamraz (Cairo), Ann Wise
(Rome).

A lightly armored Italian M-13/40 tank, serving with General Erwin Rommel's Afrikakorps, churns across the rocky Libyan Desert. Dispatched to Africa in February 1941 to shore up the Reich's faltering Italian partners, Rommel turned his outnumbered, erratically supplied army into a legendary fighting force that would challenge the British hold on the Middle East.

This volume is one of a series that chronicles the rise and eventual fall of Nazi Germany. Other books in the series include:
The SS
Fists of Steel
Storming to Power
The New Order
The Reach for Empire
Lightning War
Wolf Packs
Conquest of the Balkans
The Center of the Web
Barbarossa
War on the High Seas
The Twisted Dream

Second printing 1991. Printed in U.S.A.

Published simultaneously in Canada.
School and library distribution by Silver Burdett
Company, Morristown, New Jersey 07960.

TIME-LIFE is a trademark of Time Warner Inc.
U.S.A.

**Library of Congress Cataloging in
Publication Data**
Afrikakorps / by the editors of Time-Life Books.
    p.   cm. — (The Third Reich)
    Includes bibliographical references.
    ISBN 0-8094-6983-9
    1. World War, 1939-1945—Campaigns—Africa,
North.   2. Germany. Heer. Panzerarmeekorps
Afrika—History.   3. World War, 1939-1945—Cam-
paigns—Africa, North.   4. Africa, North—
History—1882-
I. Time-Life Books.   II. Series.
D757.55.A4A37 1990   940.54'23—dc20   89-49109

Other Publications:

TIME-LIFE LIBRARY OF CURIOUS
   AND UNUSUAL FACTS
AMERICAN COUNTRY
VOYAGE THROUGH THE UNIVERSE
THE TIME-LIFE GARDENER'S GUIDE
MYSTERIES OF THE UNKNOWN
TIME FRAME
FIX IT YOURSELF
FITNESS, HEALTH & NUTRITION
SUCCESSFUL PARENTING
HEALTHY HOME COOKING
UNDERSTANDING COMPUTERS
LIBRARY OF NATIONS
THE ENCHANTED WORLD
THE KODAK LIBRARY OF CREATIVE PHOTOGRAPHY
GREAT MEALS IN MINUTES
THE CIVIL WAR
PLANET EARTH
COLLECTOR'S LIBRARY OF THE CIVIL WAR
THE EPIC OF FLIGHT
THE GOOD COOK
WORLD WAR II
HOME REPAIR AND IMPROVEMENT
THE OLD WEST

For information on and a full description of any
of the Time-Life Books series listed above, please
call 1-800-621-7026 or write:
Reader Information
Time-Life Customer Service
P.O. Box C-32068
Richmond, Virginia 23261-2068

General Consultants

Col. John R. Elting, USA (Ret.), former associate professor at West Point, has written or edited some twenty books, including *Swords around a Throne*, *The Superstrategists*, and *American Army Life*, as well as *Battles for Scandinavia* in the Time-Life Books World War II series. He was chief consultant to the Time-Life series, The Civil War.

Williamson Murray is a professor of European military history at Ohio State University and has been a visiting professor at the Naval War College. He has written numerous articles and books on military affairs, including *The Luftwaffe, 1933-1944*, and *The Change in the European Balance of Power, 1938-1939*. He has also coedited the three-volume study, *Military Effectiveness*.

Contents

Strangers in their own land, two Libyans in *jallabiya* stand aside as panzers of Rommel's Afrikakorps advance against the British.

Bailing Out a Beleaguered Ally

The sleek, shark-nosed Heinkel 111 flew in from the sea, circled, and set gracefully down on the airstrip at Castel Benito, fifteen miles south of Tripoli in the Italian colony of Libya. It was almost noon on February 12, 1941. The twin-engine bomber taxied to a halt, a hatch opened, and down climbed a stocky officer with blue-gray eyes and a resolute chin. The twin stars on his shoulder boards proclaimed him to be a lieutenant general of the German army. His name was Erwin Rommel, and he had come to Libya on a mission that he had described to his wife, Lucie, as "big and important." It was all of that. Rommel's assignment was to prevent the British from running Germany's feckless Italian ally clear out of North Africa.

The task had been declared virtually impossible by two of Rommel's fellow generals, who had preceded him to Africa on fact-finding tours. As Rommel rode into Tripoli, Libya's capital and chief deepwater port, he could see for himself the defeat etched on the faces of Italian soldiers streaming back from the battle zone to the east. Many of them had thrown away their weapons. Rommel would soon learn that Italian officers were openly packing their bags to escape an expected onslaught by the British—who were still nearly 400 miles away. General Italo Gariboldi, the burly, white-haired Italian commander, appeared exhausted and despairing.

That afternoon, Rommel went aloft in the He 111 to "get to know the country," as he succinctly put it. North Africa was a harsh place to fight a war. Rommel stared down in fascination at a forbidding portion of the great Sahara: the sun-scorched Libyan Desert, which extends eastward for more than 1,200 miles into Egypt. Except for the Via Balbia, the Italian-built highway rimming the Mediterranean, the land was devoid of easily recognizable features as it ascended from the narrow coastal plain to a dun-colored plateau strewn with boulders. Only near the coastal towns, where Italian colonists had installed irrigation systems, was there any substantial greenery. Otherwise, wrote Rommel, the macadam road "stretched away like a black thread through the desolate landscape, in which neither tree nor bush could be seen as far as the eye could reach."

At sea to the north, Rommel could glimpse the convoy bringing in the

General Erwin Rommel inspects the first Afrikakorps units to disembark at the palm-shaded port of Tripoli in February of 1941. To his right is General Italo Gariboldi, the Italian commander in North Africa and Rommel's nominal superior.

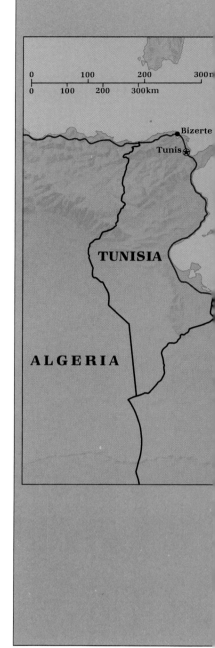

first of his troops. Before long, the officers and men of the Afrikakorps would become legends, enshrined in the pantheon of the Wehrmacht. But for now—unlike the British, with their long experience in the desert—the Germans were appallingly unprepared for what awaited them. Adolf Hitler had never contemplated fighting a colonial war, and his army had not a single unit fit for African duty. Accustomed to the moderate climate of northern Europe, the troops would have trouble coping with summer temperatures that commonly exceeded 120 degrees Fahrenheit and soared even higher when blinding sandstorms raged in from the southern Sahara. And the soldiers would have to carry every bit of sustenance with them, including most of their water, because the desert was a wasteland, lifeless except for swarms of black flies and sand fleas and the scattered prickly bushes known as camel thorn.

Yet where others saw only hostile terrain, unprepared troops, and accursed allies, Rommel saw opportunity. He was not the first tactician to find a resemblance between the desert and the sea; each possessed uncharted expanses navigable only by sun, stars, and compass. But it struck him that, just as the sea was the province of navies, so the desert would be a natural arena for tanks, ideally suited to the new tactics of swift, bold maneuver that he had mastered as a panzer-division commander in the blitzkrieg conquest of France. Soon Rommel would put his ideas to the test with such audacity and cunning that he would become known as the Desert Fox.

Rommel's arrival in Libya ended more than six months of German indecision over North Africa. The debate had begun in July 1940, when, after France fell, Hitler confronted the problem of subduing Great Britain. One possibility, favored by some in the High Command of the Wehrmacht (OKW), was to cripple the British by striking at their vital Mediterranean interests. From bases in Egypt, British and Commonwealth forces stood guard over the Suez Canal, ensured the flow of oil from the Middle East, and maintained Britain's lifeline through the Mediterranean.

Hitler, however, was thoroughly disinterested in opening a theater of operations in the Mediterranean. He chose instead to launch a direct assault on the British Isles through Operation Sea Lion—aerial bombardment to be followed by an invasion across the English Channel. The Führer was not unmindful of the Mediterranean and North Africa, but he intended to leave the south to his Italian partner, Benito Mussolini. As Rommel later noted, the Führer's intentions that summer were "Not one man and not one penny for Africa."

Mussolini, a man endowed with the instincts of a jackal, was only too pleased at the prospect of expanding his African empire while the British

Map labels:

ITALY

SICILY

GREECE · Athens

TURKEY

MALTA

Mediterranean Sea

CRETE

CYPRUS

Haifa

Cyrene · Derna

Barce

Gulf of Sirte

Benghazi · Gazala · Tobruk · Bardia · Sidi Barrani

Bir Hacheim

Sollum

Port Said

Suez Canal

Alexandria

Mersa Matruh · El Alamein

CYRENAICA

Sirte · VIA BALBIA

Agedabia

El Agheila

POLITANIA

LIBYA

EGYPT

QATTARA DEPRESSION

Nile River · Cairo · Suez

COAST ROAD

The North African battlefield, scene of General Erwin Rommel's audacious attacks and British counterstrokes, stretched for more than 1,000 miles from Libya's western province of Tripolitania across the deserts of Cyrenaica to the Egyptian border, and east from there almost to Cairo and the vital Suez Canal. Mostly a wasteland of sand and rocks, stony inland plateaus, and scorching coastal plains, the region was linked by a single highway. Back and forth on this coast road surged much of the fighting—and the endless supply caravans that sustained the opposing armies. Strung along the road, like cracked and dusty beads on a black ribbon, were the towns that gave their names to crucial battles in the seesaw desert campaign: Benghazi, Tobruk, Bardia, Sidi Barrani, Mersa Matruh, El Alamein. Washing the long African coastline was the Mediterranean Sea, also a fiercely contested battleground, where British warships and aircraft from Egypt and Malta vied with Axis planes and submarines for control of the shipping lanes.

lion was beset elsewhere. The duce had taken Italy into the war on June 10, 1940, barely two weeks before the fall of France, and was sniffing about for an easy feast. Italy already had colonies in the East African interior—in Eritrea, Italian Somaliland, and Ethiopia. From there, Mussolini's armies had invaded Kenya, the Sudan, and British Somaliland in late June. With ten divisions at their disposal and scant opposition, the Italians quickly penetrated south into Kenya and overran Somaliland, thus opening the way to the Sudan and Egypt. The prospects were enticing for a giant pincer closing on Egypt from the south and west, a pincer that would destroy the British and make Italy the foremost power in Africa north of the equator.

The key to the strategy was Libya, in North Africa. From there, the duce would launch the western arm of his envelopment. An Italian possession since 1911 and only 300 miles by sea from Sicily, Libya bordered on Egypt

to the east and the French colonies of Tunisia and Algeria to the west. The defeat of France had neutralized Libya's western neighbors and allowed Mussolini to concentrate on his main chance. On June 28, he ordered a massive invasion of Egypt, "that great reward for which Italy is waiting." And because his 250,000 troops would face scarcely 36,000 defenders, the Italian dictator was brimming with confidence.

More than six weeks passed, however, before Mussolini's forces bestirred themselves. Not until September 13 did the first Italian troops cross into Egypt. With an air of parade, 80,000 men in five divisions, shielded by 200 tanks, moved out from Capuzzo, a village two miles west of the border. A grand fanfare of silver trumpets signaled the departure, and black-shirted Fascist shock troops, theatrically armed with daggers and hand grenades, stomped off at the head of the army. In the rear rolled trucks carrying marble monuments with which to mark the triumphal progress.

As it happened, not many of the marble milestones were required. The Italian spearhead traversed the escarpment edging the Libyan plateau and descended into the Egyptian town of Sollum. Encountering little resistance from the outnumbered British units in the vicinity, the invaders moved leisurely along the narrow coastal plain, taking four days to penetrate less than sixty miles. At the village of Sidi Barrani, the Italian commander at that time, Marshal Rodolfo Graziani, halted for rest and reinforcement. Rome radio blared of victory and imaginatively transformed the cluster of mud huts into a metropolis. "Thanks to the skill of Italian engineers," the radio announced, "the tramcars are running again in Sidi Barrani."

In fact, Italian engineering skills were swiftly employed to convert the area into a defensive fortress. Instead of pressing ahead, Graziani, pleading to Rome for more men and supplies, ordered the construction of a semicircular shield of seven major strongpoints, beginning on the coast at Maktila, fifteen miles east of Sidi Barrani, and curving inland for fifty miles. These fortified camps included not only defenses but such amenities as officers' clubs that served chilled Frascati wines in fine glassware. Troops also began improving the road back to the Libyan border and constructing a 100-mile-long pipeline to bring up water. Graziani then settled comfortably down to await the tank reinforcements Mussolini had promised.

The Germans viewed all this with distaste and foreboding. The high command had long harbored doubts about Italian military capabilities, and the present conduct of war by sit-down—in contrast to the Wehrmacht's own lightning thrusts—only too clearly confirmed the suspicions. The severe attrition the Luftwaffe was suffering in the skies over England had taught Hitler respect for the Royal Air Force, and he feared that the British might bomb Italy from bases located in Egypt. Worse, there was the possibility of a major embarrassment to Axis interests in the Middle East and a vague risk that the British might threaten the southern flank of the forthcoming Operation Barbarossa, Hitler's cherished invasion of the Soviet Union. At a conference with Mussolini on October 4, the Führer offered panzers and planes to help Graziani get moving. The duce coldly rejected the offer, although he conceded that German aid might be welcome in the final stages of the campaign. Mussolini promised Hitler that the offensive would resume by the middle of the month.

What ensued instead, to Hitler's vast annoyance, was a surprise Italian invasion of Greece on October 28. Mussolini had neglected to inform Hitler out of pure spite: He meant to pay back the Führer "in his own coin"—as the duce confided to his foreign minister—for Hitler's unannounced occupation of Rumania on October 11. Enraged both at Mussolini's duplicity and because there was now a risky new theater of war, Hitler postponed any aid whatsoever to the Italians in North Africa.

The pessimistic report of one of Hitler's trusted officers influenced his decision. Major General Wilhelm Ritter von Thoma of the OKW had recently returned from an inspection of Libya. Thoma concluded that the Italians, for all their numbers, were weak and needed stiffening. But he advised that "it would be pointless" to dispatch fewer than four panzer divisions, or three more than Hitler was willing to spare from Barbarossa. Therefore, on November 12, the Führer decreed a curious compromise: German forces would be sent to North Africa only after the Italians had captured Mersa Matruh, a British coastal stronghold eighty miles east of Sidi Barrani.

Meanwhile, as the weeks of Italian lassitude stretched into months, the British forces labored industriously to strengthen their position. A narrow-gauge railway terminating at Mersa Matruh enabled them to bring forward stockpiles of supplies, men, and equipment, including the 7th Armored Division. One of the division's three regiments was equipped with Matildas, thick-skinned, thirty-ton tanks that were specifically designed to support advancing infantry. Though still outnumbered almost three to one, the British enjoyed far superior equipment and could assemble tanks, gun carriers, and trucks into the fully motorized striking columns essential for desert warfare—just as battle fleets operated at sea.

The Italian army in North Africa, as Rommel wrote later, had been designed not for modern combat but "for a colonial war against insurgent tribesmen. Its tanks were too light and their engines underpowered." The Italians themselves would soon call their M-13 tanks "rolling coffins," since they quickly overheated and were vulnerable to most enemy artillery. Moreover, the Italian army was short of antitank guns and antiaircraft batteries. Its field artillery designs dated from World War I, some poor copies of the old French 75-mm cannon that had earned lasting fame at Verdun. Many of its aircraft were obsolete. But its worst feature, wrote Rommel, was that the bulk of the army consisted of foot soldiers without transportation, a condition that made rapid maneuver impossible. The German liaison officer assigned to Marshal Graziani, Major Heinz Heggenreiner, was appalled to learn that the Italians in North Africa counted only 2,000 motor vehicles of all types. This was fewer than the number possessed by a single motorized division in the German army.

To all these shortcomings was added wretched leadership. Graziani and his chief subordinates were guilty of gross oversights. None of their strongpoints adequately supported another, and there was insufficient depth to the defenses. In constructing the fortifications around Sidi Barrani, the

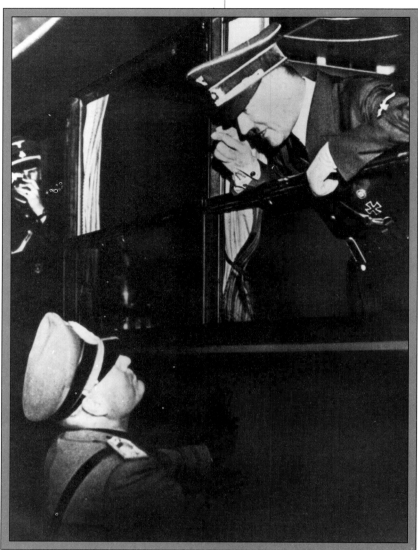

Leaning from a window of his railroad car, Hitler bids farewell to Mussolini after their October 1940 meeting at the Brenner Pass, located on the Reich-Italian border. At this meeting, the duce refused offers of German help in Africa, boasting that his armies would soon be in Cairo.

Italians had left an unprotected—and unpatrolled—gap of fifteen miles between two main positions. It was here, thirty miles from the sea, that Commonwealth forces decided to test the mettle of Mussolini's legions early in December 1940.

Planning for the attack was both meticulous and imaginative. With great secrecy, the field commander, Lieut. General Richard O'Connor, cached five days' worth of food, gasoline, and ammunition in desert cisterns between Mersa Matruh and the Italian camps. Then, on the morning of December 7, he sent his two highly mobile divisions—the 7th Armored and the Indian 4th, supported by a regiment of the 7th's Matilda tanks— forward on a front more than a mile wide. They collected the hidden supplies and spent the night in the open desert, resting for the attack.

The following day, an Italian reconnaissance plane spotted the attacking formations as they approached the Italian line. The pilot was Lieut. Colonel

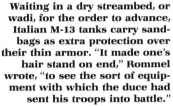

Waiting in a dry streambed, or wadi, for the order to advance, Italian M-13 tanks carry sandbags as extra protection over their thin armor. "It made one's hair stand on end," Rommel wrote, "to see the sort of equipment with which the duce had sent his troops into battle."

A column of Italian prisoners, some of them carrying suitcases, stretches to the horizon along the Via Balbia after being cut off and captured by fast-moving British motorized forces.

Vittorio Revetra, the fighter commander, and he immediately radioed Marshal Graziani at headquarters. To Revetra's astonishment, Graziani serenely told him to "let me have that in writing." Although Graziani later asserted that he passed the word to his subordinates in the field, no one attempted to do anything about the advancing enemy. That night, the British and Indians penetrated the gap between the Rabia and Nibeiwa camps and halted a few miles to the west.

Shortly after seven the next morning, December 9, the Italian defenders of Nibeiwa were brewing coffee and baking rolls for breakfast when the first Matildas burst into camp. Shells from the tanks' two-pounder guns smashed a score of M-13s parked just outside the compound. Return fire from Italian antitank guns merely bounced off the British armor. The camp commander, General Pietro Maletti, rushed from his tent with a submachine gun and went down mortally wounded, a bullet in his lung.

Other Italian officers exhibited less courage as the Allies took control of Nibeiwa and wheeled north toward the other positions. At Maktila, on the coast, a white flag went up after the first bursts of gunfire. "Sir, we have fired our last cartridge," the camp commander solemnly advised a British officer. He was standing next to a huge supply of ammunition.

Over the next three days, practically the entire Italian force in Egypt was cut off. So many Italians were surrendering—39,000 of them, including four generals—that a British battalion commander simply reported his haul as "5 acres of officers, 200 acres of other ranks." These extraordinary doings brought a change in British plans: O'Connor had originally intended only a five-day raid to test the Italians; now the probe became a major offensive.

On December 16, British tanks swept into Libya and captured Capuzzo, the springboard for the Italian invasion three months earlier. They also seized Halfaya Pass, a narrow defile in the coastal escarpment that allowed the only rapid passage into or out of Egypt. The tattered survivors withdrew into Bardia, a coastal stronghold atop a 350-foot-high cliff twelve miles from the border. The garrison comprised 45,000 men and 400 guns behind a defensive line that included a twelve-foot-wide antitank ditch and extensive minefields. The commander, Lieut. General Annibale Bergonzoli, was rated one of the better Italian officers. Sporting a fiery red beard that earned him the nickname Electric Whiskers, Bergonzoli had distinguished himself in the Spanish Civil War, and unlike most high-ranking Italians, he scorned luxury, ate and drank with his troops, and slept in a standard-issue tent. He radioed Mussolini, "In Bardia we are, and here we stay."

There Bergonzoli stayed for two weeks while the British reinforced their remaining armor and reshuffled their forces to bring the Australian 6th Division into the line. Then, at dawn on January 3, 1941, after an all-night

aerial pounding by the RAF, the Australians attacked to the accompaniment of offshore shelling from three battleships. The Aussies cracked open the Italian fortifications on a front nearly eight miles wide and by dusk the next day had mopped up the last of the defenders. Electric Whiskers Bergonzoli was not among the 40,000 prisoners taken; he had escaped to Tobruk, a port and fortress located seventy miles to the west. But Tobruk offered no sanctuary. The 7th Armored Division raced to invest the town, quickly followed by the Australians. Tobruk held out for thirty-six hours of bitter fighting before surrendering on January 22, bringing another 25,000 prisoners into the bag.

Racing along the coastal Via Balbia, the British and Australians next approached the northern apex of the bulge where Libya's eastern province of Cyrenaica protrudes into the Mediterranean. On January 25, they captured Derna, a village 100 miles northwest of Tobruk, and nearly trapped a large tank force fifty miles inland, at the old fort of Mechili. General O'Connor then took a daring gamble. Worried that the Italians might escape Cyrenaica and reach Tripoli, he sent the 7th Armored dashing 150 miles across the interior of Cyrenaica's bulge to cut off the retreating Italians. A column of 3,000 British soldiers in trucks, tanks, and scout cars departed Mechili at daybreak on February 4. The vehicles were already on the point of breakdown after a month of combat, and the desert plateau was soon littered with abandoned machines. Nevertheless, by dawn the next day, the column was nearing the oasis of Msus, only fifty miles from the coast. But O'Connor knew the sprint might be in vain; aerial reconnaissance reported that the Italians were retreating faster than expected.

On receiving this information, he detached a party of 11th Hussar armored cars and motorized infantry and sent it churning ahead. Shortly after noon, this detachment reached the coast road near the village of Beda Fomm, thirty miles south of the port city of Benghazi. The timing could scarcely have been better. Thirty minutes later, when the lead trucks of the Italian column approached from the north, they faced a brigade of British riflemen, dismounted and astride the road.

The Italians fought desperately to break through, but their fate was sealed as other British units came up. And when the Italians learned that Marshal Graziani had fled to Tripoli, white flags appeared everywhere. Along a fifteen-mile-long stretch of road, the British rounded up the remnants of an army: 20,000 prisoners brought the total to 130,000 Italians captured during the two-month campaign, along with 400 tanks and more than 1,200 guns. The British and Commonwealth forces had lost fewer than 2,000 men killed, wounded, or missing. Six Italian generals had been taken in the action around Beda Fomm alone. Among them was the elusive

The senior Italian commander captured in the British sweep across Cyrenaica was Lieut. General Annibale Bergonzoli (*center*), shown arriving in Cairo with other captive officers in February 1941. Bergonzoli's men called him Electric Whiskers because his flaming red beard seemed to give off sparks.

Electric Whiskers, who was captured when a British lieutenant stuck the barrel of a submachine gun through the window of Bergonzoli's Fiat. "You got here a bit too quickly today," the general said calmly. It was a fitting epitaph for the campaign.

At the Berlin headquarters of the OKW, senior German officers had followed the Libyan drama with mounting alarm. In December, after the British had recaptured the bases in Egypt, the Italian high command pleaded urgently for aid. Hitler responded by transferring the Luftwaffe's X Air Corps, with 100 bombers and 20 fighter escorts, to Sicily and southern Italy to protect Italian shipping and attack British convoys en route to Egypt. On January 9, after Bardia had been lost, the Führer decided to commit troops to Libya. The loss of the colony "would not entail very far reaching military consequences," he told his generals, but "the effect on Italian morale would be extremely unfavorable." His official directive two days later ordered the dispatch of a *Sperrverband,* or blocking force, to halt the British. As a result, what soon became known as the Afrikakorps was formed. The new 5th Light Division, commanded by Major General Johannes Streich and built around a nucleus from the 3d Panzer Division, was the corps's first unit.

Initially, it was to have only one tank company. The 5th Light was scheduled to arrive in North Africa in mid-February, but after the fall of Tobruk on January 22, the timetable was advanced.

Finally, on February 3, as the Italians retreated headlong toward Tripoli, Hitler reconsidered the problem of North Africa. At a meeting of his strategists devoted mainly to Operation Barbarossa, the Führer interjected the subject of the failing war in Africa. If the British took Libya, he mused, they "could put a pistol to Italy's breast" and perhaps force Mussolini to make peace. At the same time, he added, British troops might be shifted to Syria to threaten Barbarossa. As a counterweight, Hitler enlarged his commitment to Operation *Sonnenblume*, or Sunflower, as the African venture was code-named. He ordered the Luftwaffe to prepare for action in North Africa, added a panzer regiment to the 5th Light Division, and doubled the size of the embryonic Afrikakorps by approving the follow-up shipment of an entire panzer division.

The choice of Erwin Rommel to command the expedition was something of an accident. Major General Hans von Funk, a Prussian aristocrat who had commanded the 5th Panzer Regiment, was originally slated to head the new corps. But he had flown to Tripoli in January on an inspection tour and returned with such a negative report—nothing could be done; Libya was lost—that Hitler looked elsewhere for a leader. He first considered Lieut. General Erich von Manstein, the clever strategist who had devised the stunning invasion of France, but then thought better of it; Manstein would be more valuable for Barbarossa. Hitler settled for another rising star.

At the age of forty-nine, Rommel was everything the Führer admired in

Luftwaffe personnel about to leave Naples on a troopship bound for Africa pass the time playing chess and soaking up the Mediterranean sun. To avoid crippling losses should a ship be sunk, only a portion of any unit traveled on the same vessel.

a general. Though not a member of the Nazi party, Rommel presented a sharp contrast to the traditional, stiff-necked German military elite, whom Hitler detested. Further, Rommel had attached himself wholeheartedly to the new regime. Neither an aristocrat nor a Prussian, he had risen from common Swabian stock, joined the army at the age of eighteen, and won a high military honor, the Pour le mérite, or Blue Max, for extraordinary boldness and courage as an infantry commander against the Italians in World War I. Between the wars, he had written brilliantly on infantry tactics and had so impressed Hitler that he was selected to command the Führer's personal guard during the invasions of Czechoslovakia and Poland. For France, Rommel was given the 7th Panzer Division. After thirty years as an infantryman, he swiftly demonstrated his genius for blitzkrieg.

With their general leading the way in his command vehicle, the 7th Division's panzers rolled across France. They moved with such speed and daring, covering as much as 150 miles a day and unexpectedly materializing behind enemy lines, that the French referred to them as the Ghost Division. The Nazi propaganda machine seized upon Rommel as an exemplar of the new German general. But just to make certain that his mentor knew his exploits in detail, Rommel prepared a long narrative of the French campaign, illustrated it with meticulously drawn maps, and presented a copy to Hitler in December 1940.

Such an officer, the Führer decided, would be ideal to tackle a difficult command on an unfamiliar continent, and he summoned Rommel to Berlin on February 6. "I picked him," Hitler said later, "because he knows how to inspire his troops." For Rommel, an independent command, especially in that locale, was in literal truth just what the doctor ordered. "You need sunshine, General," advised the physician who was treating him for rheumatism. "You ought to be in Africa."

When Rommel arrived in Tripoli on February 12, his immediate concern was to rally the demoralized Italians. "Something had to be done at once to bring the British offensive to a halt," he wrote. After the calamity at Beda Fomm, the enemy had moved almost 100 miles westward along the highway to El Agheila, athwart the border between Cyrenaica and Tripolitania. Only 400 miles stood between the British and Tripoli.

Rommel quickly took charge, although he was subordinate to the Italian commander under the terms of a delicate agreement between Hitler and Mussolini. "Mussolini would probably like it most if the German troops fought in Italian uniforms," Hitler had quipped. The Luftwaffe had already gone around the Italians to Hitler for permission to bomb the recently lost port of Benghazi; the Italians had banned bombing because many of their

officers owned luxurious villas in the vicinity. Hitler interceded with Mussolini, and the Luftwaffe was allowed to hit the Benghazi docks.

Rommel next persuaded General Gariboldi, who had replaced Graziani, to establish a new defensive line farther east than intended—at the coastal village of Sirte, 250 miles east of Tripoli. Then, while two Italian infantry divisions and the Ariete Armored Division, with its sixty outmoded tanks, moved toward Sirte, Rommel prepared for the arrival of his Afrikakorps.

The first German units—reconnaissance and antitank battalions—disembarked on February 14. Rommel ordered them to unload their equipment under searchlights that very night, despite the risk of air attack. The next morning, in Tripoli's palm-lined plaza, he reviewed his troops as they paraded past in their olive-colored uniforms and pith helmets. (The helmets soon proved fragile and impractical and were discarded in favor of peaked forage caps that became the trademark of the Afrikakorps.) Imme-

A twenty-two-ton Mark III medium tank destined for Rommel's main armored unit, the 5th Light Division, is lowered to the dock in Tripoli in early March 1941. Squat, powerful, and maneuverable, the Mark III had a 50-mm gun that fired shells capable of penetrating British armor from up to 1,000 yards.

Rolling toward the front in February of 1941, Mark I scout tanks of the German 5th Light Division pass beneath the grandiose marble archway that Mussolini erected in the desert in 1937 to mark the border between the Libyan provinces of Tripolitania and Cyrenaica.

diately after, the units were hustled across the desert. When they reached Sirte twenty-six hours later, Rommel had already arrived in his Fieseler Storch reconnaissance plane and ordered patrols to locate the enemy.

A little more than a week later, on February 24, one such probe, seventy-five miles to the east at Nofilia, brought the first brush with the British. A column of armored cars, half-tracks, and motorcyclists of the 3d Reconnaissance Detachment clashed with British armored cars and antitank guns. The men of the Afrikakorps made their baptism of fire a successful one, destroying three British armored cars and capturing three soldiers, including an officer, without loss to themselves.

Although Rommel considered this a "good omen," he nonetheless was surprised at the lack of British activity. He had come to Libya half expecting to find the enemy at the gates of Tripoli, but he saw no evidence of a continuing British drive from their new bases in Cyrenaica. What Rommel did not realize was that on February 11, the day before his arrival, the British high command had decided to strip the army in North Africa in order to organize an expeditionary force for Greece. The situation in Greece was complex and fraught with danger for both sides. The Italian invasion had met with no more success than the strike at Egypt; though ill equipped and outnumbered, the doughty Greeks had sent Rome's legions reeling in defeat. The British prime minister, Winston Churchill, suspected—rightly, as it turned out—that in Greece as well as in Libya, Hitler would be forced to rush to the aid of his Axis ally. And Churchill himself intended to honor a longstanding promise to aid the Greeks in the event of German attack. In the resulting clash, the Germans would drive the British from the mainland, setting the stage for one of the war's bloodiest struggles thus far, on the strategic island of Crete.

Suiting Up for Desert Combat

As Italian fortunes faded in North Africa in 1940 and German intervention became probable, the army high command called on Hamburg's Tropical Institute to design a uniform and related equipment suited to Libya's harsh climate.

The resulting outfit consisted of trim shirt-and-tie uniforms made of durable olive green cotton with breeches and high boots, topped off by a sun helmet *(middle right)*. Steel helmets, painted tan in the field, were also provided. The Luftwaffe devised its own uniform—looser-fitting garments of tan cotton *(far right)*. And men of all branches received a wool greatcoat for protection against the frigid desert nights.

Once in the desert, soldiers soon modified their clothing *(right)* for comfort's sake, abandoning the flimsy sun helmet and constricting necktie. They also requested new items, such as lightweight caps, shorts, ankle boots, and loose trousers. Beginning in mid-1941, soldiers who had served for more than two months in the African theater qualified to wear an Afrikakorps cuff title *(below)*.

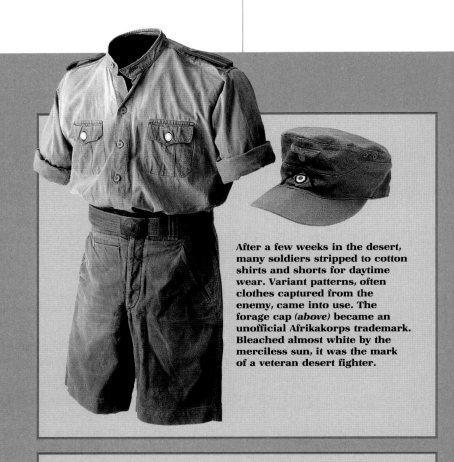

After a few weeks in the desert, many soldiers stripped to cotton shirts and shorts for daytime wear. Variant patterns, often clothes captured from the enemy, came into use. The forage cap *(above)* became an unofficial Afrikakorps trademark. Bleached almost white by the merciless sun, it was the mark of a veteran desert fighter.

This panzer officer's forage cap, identified by an inverted V of pink braid, is adorned with aluminum piping and a silver-wire eagle. The goggles protected the eyes from sand and dust.

The basic 1940 uniform bore the army's standard insignia in subdued gray, olive green, and ocher. Most accouterments, and the tops of the knee-length boots, were made of canvas webbing since leather deteriorated from desiccation and sweat damage.

The Luftwaffe's uniform for ground personnel consisted of very loose, Italian-style trousers and an open-collar tunic. The unstiffened, peaked cap (*above, left*), came with a detachable neckcloth that most wearers immediately threw away.

Yet all that mattered to Rommel at the moment was the unexpected respite. Additional units of the 5th Light Division were landing at Tripoli—Lieut. Colonel Gustav Ponath's crack 8th Machine-Gun Battalion arrived on February 25—and Rommel had time to prepare his men for desert warfare. Aside from a few frightening lectures on tropical diseases, the Afrikakorps had received no specialized training, and the units were woefully unprepared for their mission. Bakery Company 531, for example, disembarked with its wood-fired ovens to discover that the desert was virtually devoid of trees and that fuel would have to be shipped from Italy.

Desert training for the troops consisted of constant field exercises and lessons in how to navigate across featureless terrain. On their own, meanwhile, the men learned to survive the heat and cope with the clouds of clinging black flies, the voracious sand fleas, and the fine yellow dust that penetrated everything. Rommel made sure that he and members of his staff shared the soldiers' miseries. In order to harden the staff, he moved headquarters from what one officer described as the "civilized routine" of Tripoli, "which required iced lemonade through the heat of the day and smart, white uniform tunics for the informal hours of the evening," to the Spartan encampment at Sirte.

The Afrikakorps grew in numbers and desert wisdom, but Rommel could not feel comfortable until his panzers arrived. The brilliant British and Australian drive westward against the Italians, covering more than 500 miles, had proved beyond question the value of the tank in desert warfare.

To create the illusion of panzer strength, Rommel had his workshops near Tripoli create scores of wood-and-canvas dummy tanks mounted on the chassis of Volkswagens. Even after the long-awaited 5th Panzer Regiment had disembarked on March 11, bringing its complement of 150 real tanks—80 of them the more powerful Mark III and Mark IV types—he resorted to deception. Parading his armor in Tripoli the next morning to impress the local spies, Rommel made sure that the behemoths—soon to be painted the desert-camouflage shade of sand yellow—rumbled around the block several times to magnify their apparent numbers.

With the firepower of the panzer regiment's 37-mm and 50-mm cannon on hand, Rommel felt ready to take the offensive, although some units of the 5th Light Division were still en route. "Now our machine slowly starts grinding," he wrote in a letter to his wife. Rommel's orders were merely to stabilize the front, but he talked audaciously not only of recapturing Cyrenaica but of invading Egypt and driving eastward all the way to the Suez Canal, 1,500 miles distant.

Full of plans, the general flew to Berlin on March 19 to win over his superiors and secure reinforcements for a major offensive. Hitler took the occasion to award him the oak leaves for his Knight's Cross in recognition of his exploits in France. But everyone was much too preoccupied with the upcoming invasions of Greece and Russia to even consider more troops for what was regarded essentially as a sideshow.

The OKW directed Rommel, both verbally and in writing, to hold his defensive line until late May, when the 15th Panzer Division was due to arrive; after that, he might engage in limited offensive action. If successful, he could drive as far as Agedabia in western Cyrenaica, but under no circumstances was he to push the Afrikakorps beyond Benghazi.

Ever his own master, Rommel returned to the desert and immediately began disobeying orders. He approved an immediate assault against the British forward position at El Agheila, 175 miles east of Sirte. Rommel's rationale was that enemy patrols were making it impossible to supply an outpost held by a small force of Germans and Italians at Marada, ninety miles to the south. In simple fact, the restless Rommel was constitutionally incapable of remaining on the defensive; his mind was geared to attack. On March 24, a mixed force of the 3d Reconnaissance Detachment's motor-cycles, armored cars, and vehicles rolled into El Agheila and, with scarcely a shot, captured the little fort astride the Via Balbia.

So quickly did the British abandon El Agheila and withdraw to Mersa Brega, a village in the hills thirty miles to the northeast, that Rommel wondered if the enemy was as formidable as anticipated. Other signs

A Four-Pointed Slash across Cyrenaica

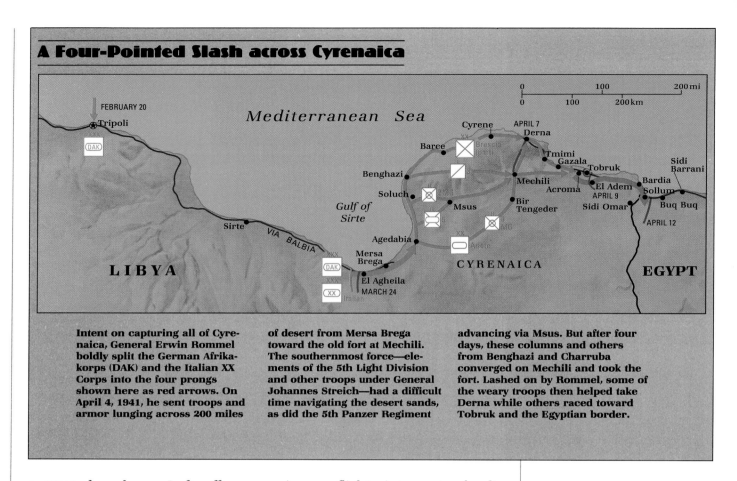

Intent on capturing all of Cyrenaica, General Erwin Rommel boldly split the German Afrikakorps (DAK) and the Italian XX Corps into the four prongs shown here as red arrows. On April 4, 1941, he sent troops and armor lunging across 200 miles of desert from Mersa Brega toward the old fort at Mechili. The southernmost force—elements of the 5th Light Division and other troops under General Johannes Streich—had a difficult time navigating the desert sands, as did the 5th Panzer Regiment advancing via Msus. But after four days, these columns and others from Benghazi and Charruba converged on Mechili and took the fort. Lashed on by Rommel, some of the weary troops then helped take Derna while others raced toward Tobruk and the Egyptian border.

suggested weakness: Luftwaffe reconnaissance flights, intercepts of radio traffic, and Rommel's own acutely sensitive feel for the battlefield—what his troops came to call his *Fingerspitzengefühl* (literally, intuition in the fingertips), or sixth sense. The Allies were even more vulnerable than Rommel sensed. In the reshuffling of forces for Greece, two crack divisions responsible for devastating the Italians had been replaced by units that were less experienced and understrength.

The British commander in chief in North Africa, General Sir Archibald Wavell, was unhappily aware of these shortcomings. The depleted Australian 9th Division, deployed around Benghazi, had been forced for lack of transport to leave one of its three brigades at Tobruk. The veteran British 7th Armored Division—actually reduced in strength to a single armored brigade on the front facing Rommel—was so short of tanks that one of its three regiments made do with captured Italian models.

Wavell was gambling that Rommel was merely engaged in aggressive patrolling, not a true offensive. What led Wavell to believe so were intercepts of top-secret radio messages between North Africa and Berlin. In a singular intelligence operation known as Ultra, the British had learned to crack the codes generated by the Enigma encryption machines and were perusing the radio traffic of the German high command. Wavell knew that Rommel had been forbidden to take the offensive until late May. And like the OKW in Berlin, he expected Rommel to obey.

Wavell could read Rommel's mail but not his mind. On March 30, a week after occupying El Agheila, the Afrikakorps attacked the new British position at Mersa Brega. Rommel later wrote that he had launched the assault

then, rather than wait for the 15th Panzer Division, because he was fearful that the foe would fortify the heights around the town.

As the 5th Panzer Regiment thrust forward, Corporal Gerhardt Klane, standing in the open turret of his tank, spotted his first "enemy" rushing wildly toward him. Klane was about to fire, but then saw that the apparition was only a terrified camel put to flight by the approach of the roaring, clanking panzers. The British were less easily impressed, and the Germans' frontal attack bogged down under heavy fire. But late in the afternoon, Rommel called in Stukas to dive-bomb the enemy artillery. He then brought forward his 8th Machine-Gun Battalion, an extra heavily armed motorized infantry unit. German sappers cleared paths through a minefield blocking the way and planted black flags to guide the trucks. Meanwhile, the 2d Machine-Gun Battalion swept through the hills in order to flank the defenders. The British abandoned Mersa Brega that evening, and the little settlement of shell-battered white houses echoed with the Afrikakorps's new battle cry—"*Heia safari!*"

The cry translated from the African Bantu language as "Drive onward!" and it perfectly suited Rommel. Two days later, on April 2, German forces under General Streich raced fifty miles to the next town on the coast highway, Agedabia. That afternoon at half past three, columns of the 5th Panzer Regiment, striking south of the road, engaged in their first heavy skirmish of the campaign when they stumbled upon a group of British Cruiser tanks cleverly concealed in Bedouin tents. The panzers swiftly recovered from their surprise and, backed by their formidable 88-mm flak guns, knocked out seven enemy tanks at a cost of three of their own. This was armor that the British could ill afford to lose, because the 2d Armored Division was now down to fewer than fifty tanks and, even without combat, was losing one tank to mechanical breakdown for every ten miles traveled.

When Agedabia fell half an hour later, Rommel was more certain than ever of his course. It was barely April, and he had already achieved the OKW's goal for early June. What was more, he had only begun his drive onward. "I decided to stay on the heels of the retreating enemy," he wrote, "and make a bid to seize the whole of Cyrenaica at one stroke."

The next day, as Rommel marshaled his forces for the thrust into eastern Libya, his nominal Italian superior, General Gariboldi, arrived in Agedabia. Gariboldi was incensed. Neither Rome nor Berlin had authorized this advance, raged the Italian. Moreover, the supply situation could not support an offensive. The two generals were arguing angrily when an orderly handed Rommel a radio dispatch. The Desert Fox glanced at it and smiled broadly. The message was from the German high command, Rommel announced triumphantly, "giving me complete freedom of action."

The order was precisely the opposite: a sharp rebuke insisting that the Afrikakorps halt its advance—right then, right there. But Rommel's bluff worked to perfection, and Gariboldi backed down. "I took the risk, against all orders and instructions," Rommel wrote his wife that April 3, "because the opportunity was there for the taking."

For his next move, Rommel cast aside conventional military wisdom that rules against a division of forces. He split his German and Italian units into four columns, each containing tanks, armored cars, and truck-borne infantry. Then he sent them racing on roughly parallel routes north and east into the bulge of Cyrenaica. The ever-active 3d Reconnaissance pushed north along the coast highway to take the abandoned port of Benghazi and then strike eastward across the desert toward the British base at Mechili. A second column—mostly the Italian motorized Brescia Infantry Division —was to follow the first to Benghazi and continue along the coast road toward Derna. Farther south, a third force, spearheaded by Ponath's machine gunners and the 5th Panzer Regiment under Colonel Herbert Olbrich, would drive across the desert toward Mechili via the oasis at Msus. The group was reinforced by antitank units and Italian infantry. The southernmost group would plunge into the heart of the desert, taking an old caravan trail to Tengeder, located forty miles south of Mechili. Rommel hoped that, by jabbing these four strong fingers rapidly forward, he could deceive the enemy as to his strength and intercept the retreating British and bring them to battle.

The desert complicated an already-difficult plan. Except for the group that stayed on the coast road, Rommel's probes faced the same brutal terrain that the British 7th Armored had struggled across two months earlier to trap the Italians at Beda Fomm. Trucks sank to their axles in the soft sand. Engines unadapted to the desert conditions overheated and seized up; others clogged with dust. A column of tanks crossing a dried-out salt marsh spied what appeared to be an enormous lake in the distance and turned back, only to learn later that it was a mirage.

Worst of all, violent sandstorms known to the Bedouins as the ghibli blew in without warning from the Sahara on winds of seventy miles per hour. The ghibli raised temperatures to 130 degrees, and clouds of fine dust cut visibility to zero. "Sand streamed down the wind-screen like water," wrote Rommel. "We gasped in breath painfully through handkerchiefs held over our faces, and sweat poured off our bodies in the unbearable heat."

Having subjected his men to these trials, Rommel watched over them like a mother hen—or eagle. When he was not with his troops, the general was circling overhead in his observation plane, rounding up lost units, and swooping down to urge his commanders onward. One morning, he mistook a column of retreating British vehicles for some of his own and nearly landed among them, his pilot pulling up at the last moment, when he and Rommel spotted the Tommies' distinctive helmets. As often as not, Rommel made his wishes known without even landing. A German motor column wearily pausing for breath looked up to see a message canister falling to earth from the Storch. The message read: "Unless you get going at once, I shall come down. Rommel."

Reports from Luftwaffe observers pinpointed what the general was looking for. Large numbers of retreating enemy soldiers were funneling into the aged Turkish-built fort at Mechili. Rommel sent orders for the three desert columns to converge there. But that was more easily said than done. Early on the morning of April 6, Rommel himself was within a dozen miles of the fort, but he had only a handful of troops with him. Despite his best efforts,

Digging out after a sandstorm had obliterated their path, the crew members of a command half-track clear the way for their vehicle and the cross-marked hospital wagon following it.

the situation had deteriorated so badly that the bulk of his forces were scattered back over the desert tracks—out of fuel, stalled by sandstorms, confused about location. Some units—notably the 5th Panzer Regiment, with most of the tanks—were out of radio range and appeared utterly lost.

Fiercely impatient when delayed, Rommel found General Streich, commander of the 5th Light Division, and ordered an attack for three that afternoon. When Streich demurred on the grounds that scarcely any of his troops had arrived, Rommel exploded. He had already reprimanded Streich twice for delays. Now, standing there steaming in his full uniform of woolen breeches and thick gray tunic while his subordinate wore cool khaki shorts, Rommel raged that Streich was a coward. In equal fury, Streich reached to his neck, indignantly unhooked the Knight's Cross he had won for gallantry in France the previous year, and threatened to hurl it at Rommel's feet unless his commander instantly withdrew the insult. Rommel muttered a halfhearted apology and mentally vowed to get rid of Streich at the first opportunity.

It was not one of Rommel's finer moments. His aides put it down to fatigue and extreme frustration, coupled with anxiety over what Berlin might say next. Yet even in the best of times, Rommel was not an easy man to get along with. "He was extremely hard," a friend later said, "not only on others but on himself as well. There was a dynamo within that never stopped humming, and because he was capable of great feats, he expected a lot from his subordinates as well, and didn't recognize that normal human beings have physical and mental limits."

Two days passed before Rommel could assemble sufficient forces to attack Mechili. Most of his troops had been exhausted by their ordeal in the desert. Rommel himself was so spent that he wrote these words to his wife on the morning of April 8: "We've been attacking for days now in the endless desert and have lost all idea of space or time."

After waiting so long, Rommel missed most of the ensuing action through a series of misadventures. He buzzed aloft in his plane to observe the battle and came under fire from a startled Italian rifle battalion 150 feet below. Fortunately, their flurry of bullets went wide—which, Rommel noted acidly, "did not speak well for Italian marksmanship." A few minutes later, Rommel landed to confer with the crew of a lone 88-mm gun, and the pilot inadvertently taxied the Storch into a sandhill, tearing up the landing gear. The chagrined artillerymen admitted that they were hoping to locate the rest of their unit; they were lost and their gun disabled. Rommel flagged down a truck, only to be held up by a sandstorm. Meanwhile, the battle was taking care of itself. Salvos from German and Italian artillery blocked all attempts by the British and Commonwealth forces to escape. Then the

infantry, supported by the few tanks on hand and by antiaircraft guns depressed to fire horizontally, stormed the fort.

When Rommel finally reached Mechili late that morning—followed by the laggard 5th Panzer—the fort had fallen and nearly 2,000 prisoners were under guard. Among the captives were seventy officers, including the commander of the 7th Armored Division, Major General Michael Gambier-Perry. And there was a fine bonus: a number of armored all-terrain command vehicles, which the British had used as mobile headquarters. Rommel immediately commandeered one of the spacious buslike machines—so large that his staff nicknamed them "Mammoths"—and discovered yet another item of useful booty: a pair of oversize goggles. Worn over the gold-braided rim of his peaked cap, the captured goggles became a distinguishing mark in photographs celebrating the Desert Fox.

That same day, April 8, Rommel motored fifty miles to Derna, on the coast, where he found another Afrikakorps triumph. Two days earlier, he had dispatched Colonel Ponath's 8th Machine-Gun Battalion to shut off the British escape route along the Via Balbia. The able Ponath, whose gunners had expended almost all their ammunition in preventing a breakout, proudly reported capturing more than 900 British combatants, including four generals. One was the commander of all British and Commonwealth troops in Libya, Lieut. General Philip Neame. Another was Neame's predecessor, General Richard O'Connor, who had come from Egypt only five days previously to oversee Neame.

The capture of O'Connor and Neame, both nabbed in an unescorted staff car after they had taken a wrong turn at night, was a telling example of how the fortunes of this curious war could shift as rapidly as the desert sands. Only two months earlier, the wiry little Irishman had led a wave of British armor westward across Cyrenaica. Now Rommel had turned the tide and was rolling eastward in a captured Mammoth very much like the one that had carried O'Connor to victory against the Italians.

Having crossed two-thirds of Cyrenaica against orders, Rommel on April 10 coolly informed his Afrikakorps of its ambitious new objective: the Suez Canal. As a first step, the Germans must seize the strategic port of Tobruk, 100 miles east of Derna. By virtue of its location astride the coast road, Tobruk commanded the lines of communication into Egypt. The town also boasted the best harbor east of Benghazi and would ease Rommel's logistics problems. His troops now consumed 1,500 tons a day in rations, water, and supplies, most of which had to be hauled 1,200 miles along the winding road from Tripoli.

For the initial pursuit to Tobruk, Rommel hastily assembled a spearhead

of 3d Reconnaissance armored cars, 8th Battalion machine gunners, and an antitank artillery battalion. To lead it, he passed over Johannes Streich and selected Major General Heinrich von Prittwitz, commander of the 15th Panzer Division, whose advance units were just beginning to disembark at Tripoli. Prittwitz was so eager for action that he had flown to the front ahead of his division. But his first taste of desert combat was his last. Shortly before noon on April 10, he was six miles from Tobruk, standing in his staff car and urging the men of his new command forward, when an antitank round slammed into the vehicle, killing the general and his driver.

Some hours later, Rommel was on a reconnaissance trip south of Tobruk when a British command car was spotted racing at breakneck speed toward the rear of his column. Rommel ordered a soldier to hold a mounted machine gun at the ready. The car was one of those General Streich's troops had captured. It slued to a halt, and out jumped Streich, shouting the news of Prittwitz's death. "How dare you drive after me in a British car!" Rommel angrily cut in. "I was about to have the gun open fire on you."

"In that case, Herr General," Streich replied tartly, "you would have managed to kill both your panzer-division commanders in one day."

If Streich had not totally alienated Rommel before, he had now. Rommel angrily ordered the general and his subordinate, Colonel Herbert Olbrich, commander of the 5th Panzer Regiment, to push on, ignoring all requests from unit commanders for rest and replenishment.

Rommel was aware that the Italians had built substantial fortifications in the area and requested a map from his allies. Inexplicably, it took a week for the Italians to furnish one, and then Rommel failed to appreciate the full strength of the defenses. The Australians had made major improvements to the semicircular thirty-mile-long perimeter, which the Italians had constructed at a radius of about nine miles from the harbor. Inside this perimeter, which was guarded by an eleven-foot-deep antitank ditch, were two concentric lines laced with mines and thickets of barbed wire. Each line was studded at 500-yard intervals with cleverly concealed concrete bunkers built flush to the ground.

These formidable defenses were held by 12,000 Australians, Britons, and Indians. Noncombatants increased the military population to 36,000. The four full brigades of Australian infantry were backed by several dozen tanks and four regiments of powerful 25-pounder guns. The troops were tough and inspired by Winston Churchill's plea that Tobruk "be held to the death without thought of retirement."

Rommel, however, was convinced that he faced a weak garrison preparing a Dunkirk-style evacuation. He sent out probing attacks, all of which suffered higher casualties than expected, then launched heavier assaults.

From the base of a rocky escarpment near Bardia, a German machine gunner scans the desert through binoculars for signs of British defenders. Rommel's 3d Reconnaissance Detachment took Bardia, a port on the Egyptian border, on April 12, after advancing 400 miles in eight days.

33

Built by Italian army engineers to foil the British, the concentric defenses around Tobruk (*map, inset*) became in the hands of crack Commonwealth troops a maddening obstacle in Rommel's path, defying all his efforts to break through it. Initial assaults by German machine gunners and panzers (*below*) were stopped by Tobruk's outer Red Line of barbed wire, antitank ditches, and concrete-shielded dugouts. An inner Blue Line— laced with minefields, more wire, and additional strongpoints mounting antitank guns, mortars, and howitzers—did an equally good job of halting Rommel's full-scale attack on April 30, 1941, after he had penetrated two miles. Adding to his woes was the forbidding terrain, an upward-sloping expanse studded with ridges and knobs that gave the defenders—many of them Australian troops renowned for their toughness—superb fields of fire. They were led by the hard-bitten Major General Leslie James Morshead, who warned his men, "There is to be no surrender and no retreat."

On Saturday, April 12, a probe by the 8th Machine-Gun Battalion and a score of panzers bogged down at the antitank ditch, which was well camouflaged by a layer of thin boards and sand. The Germans did not realize the trap was there until they were upon it. The battalion then dug in for a freezing night. On the following day, Easter Sunday, Rommel mapped out an attack by infantry and armor reminiscent of the blitzkrieg in France. He described the tactics as "concentrating strength at one point, forcing a breakthrough, rolling up and securing the flanks on either side, and then penetrating like lightning, before the enemy has time to react, deep into his rear." The attack was to begin in the predawn hours of April 13. To cover the assault, Colonel Ponath dispatched one of his motorized light flak batteries to the edge of the wire. There they would be assisted by 88s from the 18th Flak Regiment. No sooner were the guns in position than a crushing barrage from the Australian 25-pounders virtually annihilated them. With no artillery preparation, Ponath's charging men were stopped at the antitank ditch by fierce enemy fire. Again, the stubborn Germans dug in for another miserable night.

Later that night, according to plan, Ponath led 500 heavily armed troops against the center of the defensive perimeter, then infiltrated the enemy lines on a front 500 yards wide. After some confused fighting, Ponath's men established their bridgehead among the Australian bunkers, although they did not realize it because the ground-level strongpoints were impossible to discern in the dark. They reached the antitank ditch and used explosives to cave in a wide section in order to provide a crossing for panzers. Ponath also managed to bring up an antitank company.

Before dawn the next morning, with Rommel anticipating a successful climax to the battle for Tobruk, the 5th Panzer Regiment roared into action under the direction of Colonel Olbrich. The regiment deployed all the Mark III and Mark IV tanks it could still muster—scarcely 24 of 150. Following the path blazed the previous night, the panzers crossed the ditch and reached the 8th Battalion. The tank crews invited Ponath's foot soldiers to climb aboard and ride into battle. They penetrated two miles without firing a shot. Then, as dawn suffused the sky, the Germans realized that they had been lured into a trap. From front, flank, and rear, the hidden enemy opened fire, and the bridgehead became, in the words of one panzer commander, a "witch's cauldron."

The panzers furiously returned fire while the infantrymen tumbled off and scrambled for cover. The Allied gunners were so near they aimed their 25-pounders and antitank pieces point-blank over open sights. One shell ripped the turret off a big Mark IV. The German antitank crews found themselves flanked by the heavily armored Matildas. Within a few minutes,

36

Olbrich lost eleven tanks, close to half of his force, and the casualties seemed certain to continue. Olbrich ordered a fighting withdrawal.

Yet Ponath, whose icy valor in Cyrenaica had already won him the Knight's Cross, elected to stay put with his 8th Machine-Gun Battalion. About ten o'clock, the battalion beat back an Australian assault, but casualties were becoming so heavy that Ponath attempted to lead his exposed unit back to the cover of a slight rise. The colonel had gone only twenty yards when he fell, shot through the heart. At that, the battalion collapsed. Some men managed to reach safety; one of Ponath's surviving officers surrendered the rest to the Australians. Of the 500 men who had attacked that Easter Monday, only 114 evaded death or capture.

Earlier, Rommel had split off a task force of armored cars and motorized infantry with orders to bypass Tobruk and strike through the desert toward the Egyptian frontier, seventy-five miles farther east. This group, under Colonel Maximilian von Herff, quickly captured the border stations of Bardia and Capuzzo. Herff also occupied Sollum and, some time later, Halfaya Pass—key points just across the frontier in Egypt. But his group could risk no further advance as long as Tobruk remained in Allied hands, threatening the Germans' flank and rear.

The failure to crack Tobruk's hard shell over the next weeks was a bitter ration for Rommel and his Afrikakorps. The general blamed Streich and Olbrich for Easter Monday, charging that they lacked resolution. Before the end of May, both officers would be sent home "on their camels"—Afrikakorps slang for dismissal. On April 15, fresh units arrived and were immediately sent into action. In the meantime, Rommel endured his own firsthand taste of adversity on April 16, when he directed an attack against the western sector of Tobruk's defenses. He chose elements of the Italian Ariete armored and the Trento infantry divisions, stiffened by Afrikakorps officers. But the Ariete Division had already lost nearly 90 percent of its tanks to mechanical failure, and the remaining crews were smashed by the Australian guns. The Italian infantry, for its part, melted in the face of an Australian counterattack, and 800 of its men were captured.

Rommel might have anticipated the defeat. His experience against the Italians in the First World War had left him with a low opinion of their fighting caliber, and nothing seemed to have changed. As he wrote his wife, "There's little reliance to be placed on the Italian troops." Ill-trained, inadequately equipped, and poorly led, the Italian units were especially susceptible to night raids by Australians creeping silently across the stony ground in desert boots with thick crepe-rubber soles. One April morning, Rommel visited the Italian sector and was shocked to find hundreds of

discarded sun helmets, each one decorated with the black cock's feathers of a bersagliere regiment—mute evidence that an entire battalion had been taken prisoner during the night. He thereupon declared that he would execute any officer who showed cowardice in the face of the enemy.

Allies and subordinate commanders, however, were merely convenient scapegoats. Other factors underlay the failure of the Afrikakorps to take Tobruk. To begin with, the defenders outnumbered the besiegers by nearly two to one. Moreover, not since the start of the war—not in Poland, Scandinavia, the Low Countries, or France—had the German army encountered for an extended period of time an enemy so well led and so highly motivated. Finally, the Germans, having grown accustomed to the quick successes that came with blitzkrieg, lacked experience in static warfare. After the exhilaration of the race across Cyrenaica, the boredom of a siege magnified the normal hardships of the campaign. The men abhorred the brackish water, which someone said "looked like coffee and tasted like sulfur," and they groused about the dreadful diet. It lacked fruits and vegetables and even the staple German potato, which would have spoiled in the heat. The men subsisted mainly on unspeakable Italian canned beef from tins stamped with the initials *AM*, which the Germans called *Asinus Mussolini* (Mussolini's donkey) or *Alter Mann* (old man). Troops in forward positions could be provisioned only at night. All day,

Clad in shorts against the heat, German soldiers concentrate on keeping their weapons free of sand. They wear netting over their caps to ward off clouds of the ubiquitous desert flies.

these Germans lay hungry and cramped in whatever shallow trenches they could gouge in the rocky ground—at the mercy of the sun and insects and the Australian snipers, who zeroed in on the slightest movement.

The discomfort and danger eroded morale. "They already have a lot of dead and wounded in the 3d Company," a soldier wrote in his diary. "It is very distressing. In their camp, faces are very pale and all eyes downcast. Their nerves are taut to the breaking point." The only slight relief was to tune in Yugoslavian radio at night. They listened to a woman with a husky voice breathe a song called "Lili Marlene" about a soldier and his girl by the barracks gate. Precisely at nine o'clock, Radio Belgrade came on the air, and the men in their dugouts softly hummed along with the singer. Just yards away, the Australians were listening and humming, too, and for a few moments in the dark, a curious bond existed between these men fighting to the death in a godforsaken desert far from home.

Rommel faced the same perils as his troops. Twice in mid-April, he escaped death by inches: An artillery shell killed one of his subordinates as they talked, and strafing RAF fighters mortally wounded the driver of his Mammoth. But these dangers bothered him far less than the OKW's continuing distress over his generalship.

On April 27, Lieut. General Friedrich von Paulus, one of Rommel's comrades from the 1920s, arrived in North Africa, obviously on a mission for Berlin. Paulus was now a deputy chief of the high command, and he was taking valuable time out from planning the invasion of Russia. He had been sent to Libya because Rommel's conduct of the campaign had dismayed the army chief of staff, Colonel General Franz Halder. A precise and stuffy staff officer, Halder had never been enthusiastic about the Swabian upstart, who had risen as Hitler's protégé without first serving an apprenticeship in the OKW. And now Halder was convinced—as he noted in his diary— that "Rommel is in no way equal to his task." First, Rommel had brazenly disobeyed orders in sweeping recklessly across Cyrenaica. Now he was bogged down with heavy losses in front of Tobruk. Paulus, Halder concluded, was "the only man with sufficient personal influence to head off this soldier gone stark mad."

On April 30, two days after his arrival, Paulus witnessed the heaviest assault thus far against Tobruk. Rommel's objective was a prominence in the western sector known as Ras el Medauer or, simply, Hill 209, from which Australian gunners endangered the German supply line. At about half past six that evening, after artillery and Stukas had pounded Ras el Medauer, tanks and infantry—including newly arrived men of the long-awaited 15th Panzer Division—attacked north and south of the hill. They took Hill 209 from behind, then turned toward Tobruk and drove a wedge

three miles wide and two miles deep into the perimeter. During the night, combat engineers armed with flamethrowers moved forward to flush out the enemy from bypassed strongpoints.

The next morning, as artillery pounded the area, Rommel went among the captured bunkers and "crawled along like any front-line infantryman," reported an aide. But the German attack crumpled against the inner ring of defenses, and a stalemate developed over the next few days despite Rommel's attempts to feed in reinforcements. By May 4, the effort to expand the salient had cost the Afrikakorps its worst casualties of the campaign— more than 1,200 men killed, wounded, or missing. Paulus ordered Rommel to call off the attack. In fact, Paulus was so appalled by the casualties and hardships that, before he returned to Berlin, he firmly instructed Rommel to remain on the defensive until supply shortages could be alleviated.

Even Rommel was convinced at last that "we were not strong enough to mount the large-scale assault necessary to take the fortress." Privately, he

Using a metal cradle, members of a gun crew bring forward a heavy artillery shell to load into their weapon during the siege of Tobruk. The shells were shipped from Germany in straw coverings *(background)* in order to keep them from being nicked.

grumbled that his men suffered unnecessary casualties because of "their lack of training." He continued the siege of Tobruk but limited operations to patrols and artillery duels. The focus of the fighting shifted seventy-five miles eastward to the Egyptian border, where Maximilian von Herff's 6,000-man German and Italian battle group was digging in against British patrols. Rommel, listening to the radio intercepts, surmised that these probes would soon grow into a full offensive aimed at relieving Tobruk.

At dawn on May 15, the British committed fifty-five tanks and two brigades of infantry to the attack. Herff conducted a skillful fighting retreat from Halfaya Pass, Sollum, and Capuzzo. Enemy tanks penetrated all the way to Sidi Azeiz, a dozen miles inside Libya, but there they met stiffening opposition. For once, Italian troops fought so bravely that they won praise from a German officer. "They held out to the end against the enemy," Herff wrote, "and knew how to die without fear."

The tide of battle turned for the Germans the following morning. The 1st Battalion of the 8th Panzer Regiment, and a flak battery sent forward by Rommel reached Sidi Azeiz, and Herff, with fifteen remaining tanks, pulled off a surprise counterattack on the enemy's flank at Sollum. The British, having lost eighteen tanks, retired southeast to Halfaya Pass on the afternoon of May 16. That was the end of it. The offensive—code-named Brevity—lasted scarcely two days, and all the British had to show for their losses was the recapture of Halfaya Pass. They would not have that for long.

If Rommel permitted his opponents to hold the high ground at Halfaya, his forces outside Tobruk would be left vulnerable to attack from the rear. Equally important, Halfaya represented the principal passage for armor in either direction across the 500-foot-high escarpment separating the Egyptian coastal plain and Libya's desert plateau. Thus, in typical fashion, on the night of May 26, Rommel again sent Colonel Hans Cramer's 8th Panzer Regiment and its support elements in a deep loop around the pass and attacked from the southwest, while a battalion of the 104th Infantry Regiment staged a frontal assault from the northeast. The foot soldiers, under the inspiring command of Captain Wilhelm Bach, a fifty-year-old Evangelical minister from Mannheim, charged up the serpentine road and engaged the defenders in hand-to-hand combat. A few hours later, they reached the top of the pass and linked up with the panzers thrusting from the opposite direction.

It was Tuesday, May 27, scarcely fifteen weeks since Erwin Rommel had first glimpsed the expansive North African desert. During that span, his Afrikakorps had rescued its Italian allies and driven more than 1,000 miles eastward. Now, having regained Halfaya Pass, the Germans stood at the gateway to the heart of Egypt. ✠

The Forging of a Desert Legend

No military figure in the Third Reich was more celebrated than General Erwin Rommel, Germany's Desert Fox. A dynamic, courageous, and inspirational leader, he embodied the spirit of blitzkrieg that had carried the Wehrmacht to smashing victories in the first two years of war. As for his role in North Africa, an admiring subordinate described him as the "very soul and driving force of the German struggle."

Rommel augmented his military gifts with a theatrical flair. His image was carefully self-cultivated: The scarf, the leather greatcoat, and the British goggles strapped to his peaked cap made him a dashing and photogenic figure. The Afrikakorps commander became the darling of the Nazi news media. Although a fellow general noted sardonically that Rommel "seldom went anywhere without a posse of personal photographers," Joseph Goebbels praised Rommel's awareness of the "vital importance of combat propaganda" and approved the assignment of a senior Propaganda Ministry official to his staff.

Rommel's exalted reputation became a matter of rising concern to Allied commanders, whose men regarded the Desert Fox as a military superman. In March 1942, Sir Claude Auchinleck, the British commander in North Africa, addressed the problem in a memorandum to his senior officers. "There exists a real danger," he wrote, "that our friend Rommel is becoming a kind of magician or bogeyman to our troops. I wish you to dispel by all possible means the idea that Rommel represents something more than an ordinary German general." Even Winston Churchill was driven to distraction by Rommel's aura of invincibility. "Rommel! Rommel! Rommel!" the prime minister exclaimed. "What else matters but beating him?"

Rommel granted frequent interviews to war correspondents (*above*).

In May 1941, he appeared on the cover of the magazine *Signal (inset)*.

Signal
D Nr. 10
2. MAI-HEFT 1941

Disdaining the safety of the rear and distrusting "reports received secondhand," Rommel inspected the front lines every day to obtain the "grasp of the battlefield" that he believed was essential to victory.

"During his visits to the front, he saw everything," one of Rommel's officers recalled. "When a gun was inadequately camouflaged, when mines were laid in insufficient numbers, or when a standing patrol did not have enough ammunition, Rommel would see to it."

As his aircraft, a single-engine Fieseler Storch, idles at left, a pith-helmeted Rommel confers with the officers of a motorized column. He often piloted the observation plane himself.

Wearing his trademark leather greatcoat, Rommel issues orders from atop one of the half-dozen rugged vehicles that made up his mobile headquarters.

After a three-day battle in May of 1941, Rommel *(foreground)* commends a combined force of German and Italian troops for their defense of Halfaya Pass.

Rommel talks with an enlisted man in Tobruk shortly after the town's capture in June of 1942. "I owe everything," the general declared, "to my soldiers."

Making the Troops Feel Immortal

"Above all," Rommel preached, a commander "must try to establish personal and comradely contact with his men." Through such "skillful psychological handling, the performance of troops can be increased enormously," he wrote.

To that end, the Desert Fox made a point of circulating among the common soldiers, sharing their food, their hardships, and their dangers. "The general feels the urge to meet the men who are face to face with the enemy," one staff officer noted. "He has to speak with them, crawl forward to them in their foxholes, and have a chat with them." The result was a spiritual bonding between the men of the Afrikakorps and their leader. "He knew," wrote Major Friedrich von Mellenthin, Rommel's operations officer, "how to make them feel somehow immortal."

Lightly clad in the desert heat, Rommel leaps from a captured Crusader Mark I tank. The forty-nine-year-old general insisted that he felt "enormously fit."

Setting an Unsparing Pace

Constantly on the move, Rommel seemed indefatigable. "He had the strength of a horse," noted an officer who had been a champion skier. "He could wear out men twenty or thirty years younger."

Privately, however, Rommel conceded that his grueling itinerary "makes demands on one's strength to the point of bodily exhaustion." He endured bouts with jaundice and fever and was plagued by chronic gastritis. "The men knew that Rommel was the last man Rommel spared," a staff officer recalled. Concerned for his welfare, the soldiers supplemented his Spartan diet with fruit, vegetables, and poultry that they purchased from local Arabs.

Rommel's staff members, many of them half his age, scramble to keep up with the general

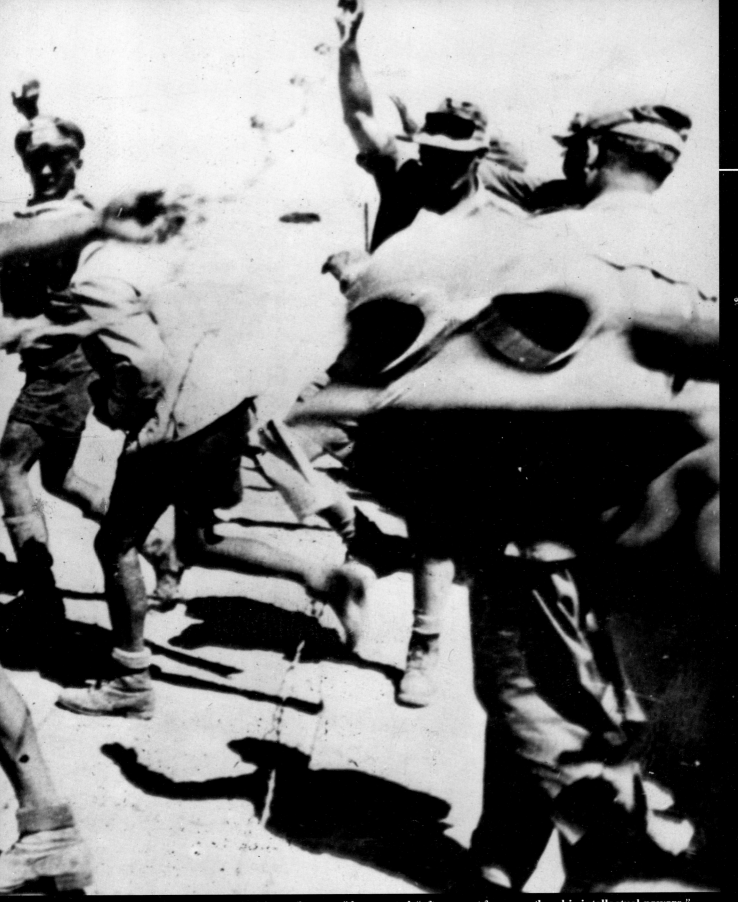

during a tour of the front. "A commander's drive and energy," he asserted, "often count for more than his intellectual powers."

TWO

Slugfest in a Sea of Sand

1

ieut. General Erwin Rommel wasted no time savoring his stunning defeat of General Sir Archibald Wavell's ill-timed Operation Brevity. He still faced the dual problem of maintaining the siege of Tobruk while preparing to fend off fresh British thrusts out of Egypt. But he was confident of ultimate success. "It is clear that the enemy will soon undertake a new offensive," Rommel said. "He will find us ready to defeat him."

For the first time in almost two years of war, a large German force was preparing to fight a defensive battle. Using lessons learned during his fruitless attacks on Tobruk in April and May of 1941, Rommel threw himself into fortifying a series of strongpoints running along the Egyptian border from Sollum, on the Mediterranean coast, across twenty miles of desert to Sidi Omar. He decided to anchor the frontier defensive line with a fortified position at Halfaya Pass, which commanded both the coast road leading to Sollum and the escarpment separating Egypt's coastal plain from the Libyan Desert. Rommel ordered the foot of the pass heavily mined; he ringed the upper, or southern, end with artillery and antitank guns dug into camouflaged firing pits.

One of Rommel's units was armed with the new, long-barreled 50-mm antitank gun. It boasted a highly accurate sight and a simple firing mechanism that recruits could learn to use quickly. But the cornerstone of Halfaya's defenses was a handful of 88-mm antiaircraft guns (pages 86-93), emplaced with their barrels horizontal to the ground. These powerful flak guns fired armor-piercing or high-explosive ammunition, and their sights had tinted lenses that enabled the gunners to aim comfortably, despite the glare of the desert sun.

An Italian battery and an assortment of captured weapons, including some recaptured Italian artillery pieces, further strengthened the Halfaya defenses. When General Italo Gariboldi, Rommel's nominal superior, objected to the use of the scavenged Italian weapons without his permission, Rommel icily ignored him. "A substantial number of these guns were put in order by German workshops," Rommel later wrote. The Italians "had been perfectly content up until then to stand by and watch this material

A British gun crew fires its 25-pounder into the night at the beginning of Operation Crusader in November 1941. A Scottish officer described the ensuing battle as a "new kind of fighting, in which the enemy would rarely be seen except as a smear of dust on the skyline."

A sign made of stones *(lower right)* in Axis-held Halfaya Pass warns RAF pilots of the presence of British prisoners. The pass was one of the few places where vehicles could drive from the coastal plain up the 500-foot escarpment to the desert.

go to wrack and ruin, but the moment the first guns had been made serviceable on our initiative, they began to take notice."

Rommel vested command of Halfaya in Captain Wilhelm Bach, the pugnacious former parson whose battalion had taken part in the recapture of the strategic position at the end of May. Rommel ordered similar fortifications built along the plateau extending westward from the pass. The new line included positions known as Point 206, about five miles south of the village of Capuzzo, and Point 208, on Hafid Ridge overlooking Capuzzo's southern flank. If Bach's German and Italian troops could hold Halfaya Pass, the other strongpoints would force the British armor to swing into the desert in a wide arc.

Rommel assigned primary responsibility for the frontier defenses to the 15th Panzer Division, with eighty tanks under Major General Walther Neumann-Silkow. He placed his other armored division, the 5th Light, led by Major General Johann von Ravenstein, south of Tobruk. From there, it could strike toward either the Sollum front or Tobruk as circumstances required. Most of Rommel's armor, which totaled 249 tanks, including some 150 obsolete Italian M-13/40s, was engaged in the investment of Tobruk. His main worry, however, was not numbers but the availability of fuel. He predicted that "our moves will be decided more by the petrol gauge than by tactical requirements."

During the first week in June, Luftwaffe reconnaissance pilots sighted large troop movements behind the British lines, and by June 14, Rommel knew from monitored enemy radio communications *(pages 58-59)* that the attack was coming the next morning. He placed all units on alert, and to forestall any aggressive moves by the Tobruk garrison, he began an artillery bombardment of the city at moonrise that night. Rommel's battle order was terse and to the point: "Halfaya will be held and the enemy beaten."

The British and Commonwealth forces were neither so well prepared nor so confident. Despite the failure of Operation Brevity, General Wavell, whose advances against the Italians during the winter had been hurled back to his doorstep by Rommel in April, was under severe pressure from his superiors in London. Winston Churchill, declaring that "those hun people are far less dangerous once they lose the initiative," demanded that "Rommel's audacious force" be destroyed. The British prime minister demonstrated his seriousness by ordering a convoy laden with tanks and airplanes to sail to Alexandria through the Mediterranean, rather than by the slower, safer route around the Cape of Good Hope and through the Red Sea. One of the ships was lost to a mine in the Strait of Sicily and another was damaged by a torpedo, but the supply convoy arrived in mid-May otherwise intact. Its cargo included 43 Hurricane fighter planes, 82 Cruiser

tanks, 21 light tanks, and 135 of the heavily armored Mark II infantry tanks that were known as Matildas.

The German conquest of Crete a few weeks later lent more urgency to Churchill's proddings. The occupation of the Greek island worried the British high command, because it put the Germans in position to establish a new line by sea to Cyrenaica. To avoid this ominous possibility and to be able to continue bombing Axis ships headed for Tripoli and Benghazi, the British needed a decisive victory.

Wavell dutifully began to plan an offensive code-named Battleaxe, but he was not at all sure that it was the right thing to do. The thirty-ton Matildas, he reported on May 28, were "too slow for a battle in the desert," and the faster fourteen-ton Cruisers had "little advantage in power or speed over German medium tanks." Moreover, all of the new armor needed to have sand filters and other special equipment installed before it would be ready for desert warfare. These modifications would not be complete until June 10. Wavell allocated a mere five days after that for training—not nearly enough time for the tank crews to gain confidence in their new machines and develop the driving, navigation, gunnery, and communication skills necessary to take on the experienced Germans.

Wavell placed Lieut. General Sir Noel Beresford-Peirse in command of Operation Battleaxe. The plan called for the VIII Corps, with 190 tanks, to launch a three-pronged attack that would destroy Rommel's forces in the Sollum-Halfaya area, relieve Tobruk, and drive the Axis troops as far west as possible *(map, next page)*. On the right wing, the Indian 4th Division, under Major General Frank Messervy, would send the Indian 11th Infantry Brigade and one and a half squadrons of Matilda tanks from the 4th Armored Brigade to retake Halfaya Pass. Simultaneously, a center column, consisting of the remainder of the Indian 4th Division and the 22d Guards Brigade, would move across the desert plateau and swing right to attack the Germans at Point 206 and Capuzzo. On the left wing, the 7th Armored Brigade, part of Sir Michael O'Moore Creagh's 7th Armored Division, would advance to Hafid Ridge with units of the divisional Support Group. The remainder of the group would move to a position twenty miles southwest of Halfaya Pass, and shield the left flank of the attacking forces.

From the outset, Operation Battleaxe promised to be a command-and-communications nightmare. The newly constituted VIII Corps was not a well-trained or cohesive whole, and many of its units had been plucked from their regular commands. To make matters more difficult, the Matilda tanks moved much more slowly than the Cruisers, and the armored and infantry units could not communicate effectively with each other. And unlike Rommel, who liked to stay close to the action so that he could adapt

The Blunting of Operation Battleaxe

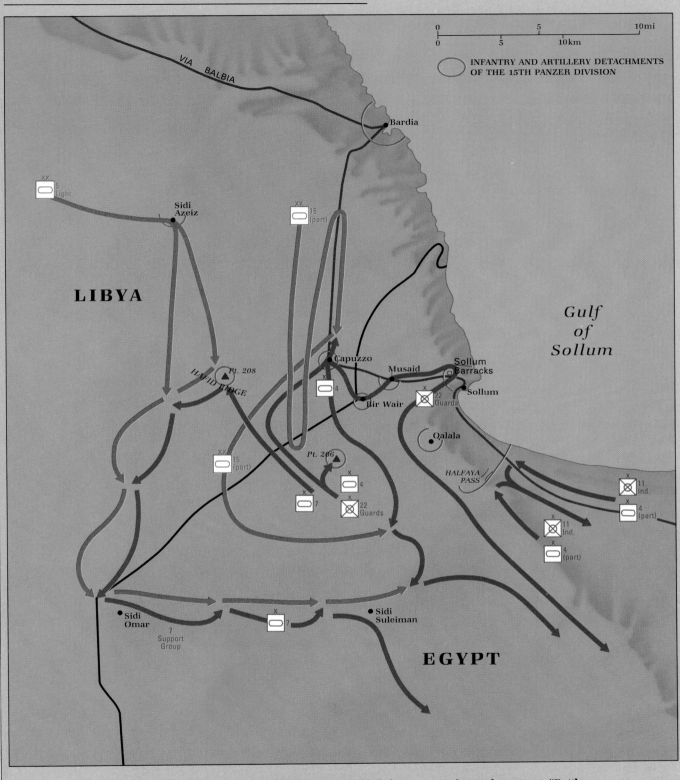

INFANTRY AND ARTILLERY DETACHMENTS
OF THE 15TH PANZER DIVISION

VIA BALBIA

Bardia

LIBYA

Sidi Azeiz

XX 5 Light

XX 15 (part)

Gulf
of
Sollum

Pt. 208

HAFID RIDGE

Capuzzo

Musaid

Sollum Barracks

Sollum

Bir Wair

22 Guards

Qalala

XX 15 (part)

Pt. 206

HALFAYA PASS

4

7

22 Guards

4

11 Ind.

11 Ind.

4 (part)

4 (part)

Sidi Omar

7 Support Group

7

Sidi Suleiman

EGYPT

In three days of June 1941, Rommel's forces *(red)* smashed the offensive code-named Battleaxe, launched by Wavell's British and Commonwealth army *(blue)*. Axis strongpoints at Halfaya Pass and Hafid Ridge stymied the British right and left wings. Wavell's center column penetrated as far as Sollum before the menacing flanking movements of the 15th Panzer and 5th Light triggered a retreat. "Battleaxe was a sorry affair," noted an observer. "The name was symbolic, for it achieved about as much as that ancient weapon would have in a modern battle."

to new situations, Beresford-Peirse chose to locate his headquarters at Sidi Barrani, sixty miles—or five hours' driving time—from the Libyan border.

In their well-prepared positions above Halfaya Pass, Captain Bach and his men waited through the night, enduring the merciless attacks of sand fleas and snatching what rest they could in their sweat-stiffened clothes. Assisted by the light of a full moon, the lookouts peered into the desert, listening to its ringing silence, punctuated now and again by the howling of jackals. Moonlight became sunlight with typical desert abruptness at four o'clock, and with the first shimmers of heat and droplets of sweat came the sound of engines and a distant cloud of dust.

Nerves stretched taut as the rumbling masses hove into view. Then the shriek of incoming shells announced the opening of the enemy artillery bombardment. The rate of fire and concentration were impressive—but the first shells plowed only empty ground. Secure in their bunkers, Bach's men watched as the enemy tanks paused and infantrymen of the Indian 11th Brigade clambered down from their trucks and formed up. Soon the tanks rumbled forward, followed by the foot soldiers. On and on they came, and the waiting verged on the intolerable before Bach at last gave the order to fire. The 88s spoke with a volume and authority the Indian troops had never experienced before. Immediately, the other antitank guns joined in. Several of the Matildas spouted smoke and slued to a stop as they shed tracks, turrets, and shards of metal. The Indian infantrymen behind the wrecked tanks tried to advance, but in the hail of fire it was impossible. British guns located the Italian battery and concentrated on it but could not silence it. Meanwhile, the German batteries continued the barrage, forcing the enemy to retreat. Of the twelve tanks engaged, Bach's men knocked out eleven.

The rest of the Indian 11th Brigade and its supporting tanks advanced against the northern end of the pass, on the coastal plain. Here the Germans relied on mines and did not have the comfort of massed guns. They, too, had to watch the advance of British tanks—six of them. Then the machines lumbered into the minefield. Four of the six Matildas blew up before they could spin around and retreat.

Captain Bach and his men had held the pass. Elsewhere, the defenders were achieving mixed results. Dug into Hafid Ridge on the desert flank, four 88s and the new 50-mm guns checked the advance of the British 7th Armored Brigade, foiling three attacks and destroying many tanks. But on the escarpment in the center, General Messervy's forces overran Point 206 and took Capuzzo after heavy fighting. Worried about a possible British breakthrough to Bardia and Sollum, Rommel ordered the 5th Light Division forward to Sidi Azeiz to be ready to counterattack.

Captain Wilhelm Bach *(in the white shirt)* oversees the emplacement of a captured British field gun at the foot of Halfaya Pass. "Bach ran his sector more efficiently than many professional officers ran theirs," a member of Rommel's staff said of the fifty-year-old reservist.

At the end of the day, Rommel pieced together a clear picture of the battle from the reports of his commanders and radio intercepts. That night, he came up with a bold plan. While the 15th Panzer Division counterattacked Messervy's forces at Capuzzo, the 5th Light Division would advance on Sidi Omar, wheel east to Sidi Suleiman, and drive to Halfaya Pass, cutting the British line of communications. "I planned to concentrate both armored divisions suddenly into one focus," Rommel later explained, "and thus deal the enemy an unexpected blow in his most sensitive spot."

At dawn on June 16, the 15th Panzer launched its counterattack against the 22d Guards and 4th Armored Brigades at Capuzzo but was forced to disengage following five hours of savage fighting, after it had lost fifty of its eighty tanks. By midday, British forces had overrun Musaid, located halfway between Capuzzo and Sollum, and were threatening Bardia. But there the offensive petered out. The best-equipped British tank-repair shops were positioned far to the rear, and the sparsely equipped regimental repair teams were overwhelmed. By contrast, the German panzer units kept their mechanics close to the action. They completed emergency repairs on their damaged tanks and hustled them back into the fray much faster than the British.

By nightfall, Messervy was increasingly worried about his left flank—and with good reason. While his 4th Armored was more than holding its own against the 15th Panzer, the 7th Armored Brigade and the units of the Support Group were driven back by the German 5th Light Division in a

Framed by the loop of an Italian radio antenna, Rommel studies Allied positions through a telescope. When at the front, he relied on radio—often small, short-range models—to stay in touch with his headquarters.

The aerial on this communications car enabled the Germans to send and receive data over extended distances. Intercepted messages were relayed to the Signals Intercept Staff for translation and evaluation.

"The Enemy Is Listening"

Imprinted on German army radios was the warning *Der Feind hört mit* —The enemy is listening. Radios became vital tools in the mobile warfare practiced in North Africa, but they had a dangerous flaw: Anyone with a receiver could listen in.

The nature of desert war led scattered units to call one another for information and reassurance. The Germans tried to instill radio discipline—eliminating extraneous traffic, keeping messages terse, and using coded or arcane language—but were not entirely successful, and their opponents even less so. The soldiers of the British Eighth Army often broadcast important information in the clear, and their careless chatter could be most revealing.

Rommel's Signals Intercept Staff, equipped with powerful receivers, assembled intelligence on the enemy's location, strength, and intentions from overheard conversations. Rommel regularly used this information to his advantage.

Inside a headquarters van, Signals Intercept personnel compile intelligence reports for immediate appraisal by Rommel's staff.

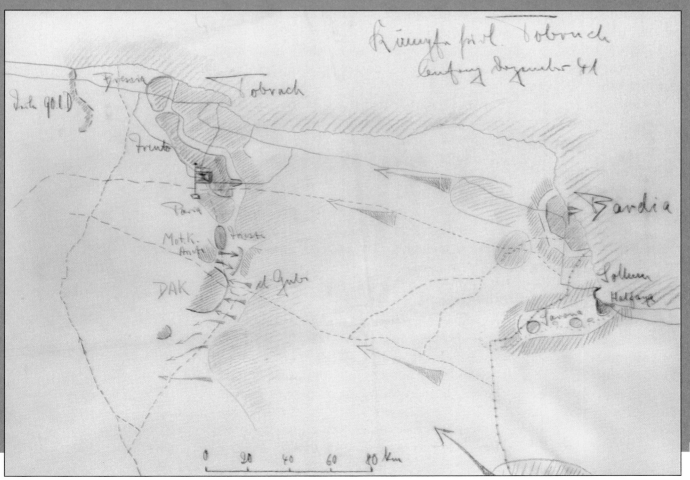

In December 1941, Rommel sketched this map of the forces between Tobruk and Bardia, based on current radio reports.

violent tank battle that zigzagged through the desert from Hafid Ridge southwest toward Sidi Omar.

Like a judo expert who instantly senses when a sudden shift of weight will send his opponent hurtling to the mat, Rommel made his move. "This was the turning point of the battle," he later wrote. "I ordered the 15th Panzer Division to disengage all its mobile forces as quickly as possible and, leaving only the essential minimum to hold the position north of Capuzzo, to go forward on the northern flank of the victorious 5th Light Division toward Sidi Suleiman."

In addition to surprise, much of the subsequent German success was attributable to a bold new tactic: Instead of fighting tank against tank, the panzer divisions opposed the British armor with antitank guns pulled by half-tracks—the cumbersome 88-mm guns jounced along in specially designed trailers. On contact with the foe, the drivers stopped, and the gunners set up their weapons and fired with deadly effect.

In the early morning of June 17, the 5th Light Division's vanguard pushed into Sidi Suleiman. By now, Creagh's force had been reduced to twenty-two Cruiser and seventeen Matilda tanks and was in danger of being overrun. As the day wore on, Rommel's Signals Intercept Staff picked up a torrent of radio reports from the anxious British, who complained of serious fuel and ammunition shortages. While the British were successfully defending their front, the Germans were cutting across their rear. Rommel expected nothing less than total victory. His two panzer divisions would sweep around the British flank and trap the entire VIII Corps.

Around noon on June 17, Beresford-Peirse and Wavell flew to Creagh's headquarters near Halfway House, about twenty miles southeast of Sidi Suleiman, hoping to rally the 7th Armored in a counterattack. But the situation was beyond salvaging. Messervy, correctly sensing that his troops at Capuzzo and Halfaya were about to be trapped, had already recalled the Indian 4th Division, on his own responsibility. The news stunned Wavell. He canceled his order for the 7th Armored to attack and called for a complete withdrawal. On reflection, Wavell agreed that Messervy's decision had been a wise one, even if it had been made without approval from above. In fact, the retreat saved the VIII Corps. In the three-day battle, British and Commonwealth casualties totaled fewer than 1,000 men. But if the soldiers' lives had been saved, their morale had been shattered. Moreover, the armored units were in shambles; Operation Battleaxe had cost the British ninety-one tanks. German losses amounted to approximately twenty-five tanks.

For some time, the dispirited British desert forces could not fathom why so many of their tanks had been destroyed. Only afterward did their

An Italian artillery lieutenant *(foreground)* and his German counterpart follow enemy movements on the Sollum front. Rommel had a generally low regard for Italian officers and supported them with Germans whenever possible.

analysts conclude that the German antitank guns were the true enemy. They were, wrote Field Marshal Sir Michael Carver, "boldly and aggressively handled as offensive weapons in the forefront of the battle, alongside or even in front of the tanks." Foremost among the antitank guns had been the fearsome 88. "Its range was colossal, and it seldom missed its target," another British officer declared. "Nearby tank commanders would see a furrow in the sand streaking toward one of their neighbors. This was made by the shell as it sped a few feet above the ground. A miss would hit the ground and then go shuddering and skipping away down the desert, still able to kill or maim anything in its path. A direct hit felt as though a gigantic sledgehammer had struck the tank. The shell made a neat, round hole about four inches in diameter and then filled the turret with red-hot chunks of flying metal."

For Wavell, the defeat—in a battle that he had undertaken against his better judgment—was a melancholy end to a long career. His message to the British high command was unflinching: "I regret to have to report that Battleaxe has failed." For Prime Minister Churchill, it was a bitter reversal of fortunes. "Rommel," he lamented, "has torn the new-won laurels from Wavell's brow and thrown them in the sand." But it was Churchill who removed the laurels. On June 22, he informed Wavell that he was to trade

places with General Sir Claude Auchinleck, the commander in chief of British forces in India.

The battle that wrecked Wavell's career made Rommel's. It represented the first decisive victory for his panzer corps against an enemy of equal size. In addition, it confirmed that his initial successes had not been sheer luck and that his bold tactics and hands-on style of leadership worked. Rommel spent three days after his victory touring the battlefield, congratulating the men. At Halfaya Pass, he praised the stalwart Captain Bach especially and recommended that he be awarded a Knight's Cross and promoted to the rank of major. The legend of Erwin Rommel was growing, and his men had boundless faith in their commander. As his young aide-de-camp, Lieu-

From his turret, a German tank commander *(right)* watches an enemy truck burn. When moving by day, both sides dispersed their tanks and other vehicles to reduce the chance of detection.

German tanks rumble past smoking enemy armor during the Afrikakorps's drive to the Egyptian border in June of 1941. Rommel observed that "great numbers of destroyed British tanks littered the country" through which his army passed.

tenant Heinz Schmidt noted, "Everywhere that Rommel went now, the troops beamed at him. He was in the process of becoming a hero."

During the lull that followed the battle for Sollum, while the German high command immersed itself in the invasion of the Soviet Union, Rommel used his new status to try to consolidate his authority in North Africa. It had been annoying enough that he was technically under the command of the Italian general, Gariboldi. Now he protested the presence in Tripoli of yet another layer of military bureaucracy: German Lieut. General Alfred Gause and a large staff had flown in on June 11 to serve as liaison between the Afrikakorps and the Italian Comando Supremo in Rome. General Gariboldi also objected to Gause, viewing his presence as a loss of prestige. Benito Mussolini's response was to sack Gariboldi in favor of a stronger personality—General Ettore Bastico.

Meanwhile, events in Berlin were about to shape the course of affairs in North Africa. Optimistic about the Reich's chance of success in the imminent Russian campaign, Adolf Hitler developed a grandiose scheme. He envisioned a converging assault on the British positions in the Middle East: from Libya into Egypt, from Bulgaria via Turkey, and through the soon-to-be-conquered Caucasus. The Afrikakorps's original mission as a blocking force in Libya was for the moment superseded.

Once the army high command learned of Hitler's interest in invading Egypt, the senior generals gave up trying to restrain Rommel and instead arranged his elevation. Nothing could be done about the nominal Italian oversight, but in an August 15 reorganization, Rommel, who had been promoted to panzer general, was given overall command of a newly constituted Panzergruppe Afrika. General Gause became Rommel's chief of staff, and the officers sent with him became Rommel's operational staff. Rommel's new panzer group would have two sections. First was the Afrikakorps, under Lieut. General Ludwig Crüwell. It now comprised two trusty armored divisions, the 15th and 21st Panzer (the 5th Light was renamed the 21st), and two infantry divisions, the newly constituted Afrika Division (later called the 90th Light) and the Italian Savona Division. The Afrika Division was made up of former members of the French Foreign Legion, Rommel's only sizable reinforcements. The second section was the Italian XXI Corps, consisting of four infantry divisions. Bastico, in addition to his title of commander in chief, would also command the new Italian XX Corps, which included the Ariete Armored and the Trieste Motorized Divisions under General Gastone Gambara.

Rommel's relationship with his new Italian superior began poorly. Shortly after Bastico's arrival, he summoned Rommel to Cyrene, 200 miles away,

for an introductory meeting. After an all-day journey, made "in vehicles riddled with bullet holes and covered with the accumulated dirt of months in the desert," as Heinz Schmidt told the story, the general presented himself at the headquarters of the *comandante superiore*. In contrast to the battered little house that served as Rommel's headquarters in Bardia, he found Bastico ensconced in a lavishly appointed, marble-pillared villa. The Italian general kept the dusty, sweaty Rommel cooling his heels in an antechamber for half an hour. "When Rommel left Bastico's office after a short talk, he was in ill humor," recalled Schmidt with wry understatement. "Thereafter, we always referred to Bastico as 'Bombastico.' "

Throughout the summer and fall, Rommel waited in vain for the substantial reinforcements and supplies that he had been promised in order to carry out the reduction of Tobruk and the invasion of Egypt as part of Hitler's grand plan. Of those that were sent, few successfully ran the 300-mile Mediterranean gauntlet between Sicily and Tripoli. British naval and air forces, operating out of Malta and alerted to routes and departure times by the super secret radio-decoding operation named Ultra, devastated Axis convoys. Between July and October, the Royal Navy and RAF sent forty ships to the bottom, along with far more matériel than had been lost in combat. Originally, Rommel hoped to attack Tobruk in September. But by the end of that month, according to Colonel Fritz Bayerlein, then chief of staff of the Afrikakorps, "only a third of the troops and a seventh of the supplies that we needed had arrived. This was a terrible handicap in our race for time with the British." Rommel simply could not compete for attention with the Russian front, where the Wehrmacht was consuming vast quantities of matériel. "For the moment, we are only stepchildren," he complained in a letter home, "and must make the best of it."

In spite of his shortages, Rommel prepared to capture Tobruk, and strengthened his defenses along the Egyptian border. He selected jumping-off points for the attack on Tobruk and targeted his artillery on the fortress. Tirelessly, he crisscrossed the desert, shuttling between siege lines and the frontier outposts, frequently showing up unannounced to oversee the buildup of fortifications and study the latest situation reports. "Nothing escaped him," one of his staff officers declared. "While very popular with young soldiers and noncommissioned officers, with whom he cracked many a joke, he could be very offensive to commanders if he did not approve of their measures."

Everywhere he went, Rommel pounded home the idea that each strongpoint must consider itself a self-contained fortress. Even if the panzers disappeared for days or weeks, the men had to hold out and believe that the panzers would return and rescue them. The anchor of his defenses

would again be the strongpoints at Halfaya Pass and around Capuzzo. Rommel ordered the twenty-mile stretch from Sollum to Sidi Omar extensively mined and assigned the Italian Savona Division to defend it, supported by German artillery detachments equipped with 88-mm guns. He placed two German reconnaissance units along his desert flanks between Sidi Omar and Bir el Gubi, more than thirty miles south of Tobruk. The Italian Trieste Division was at Bir Hacheim, thirty miles west of Bir el Gubi, where the Italian Ariete Armored Division was stationed. A semicircle of fortifications behind the border defensive line protected Bardia. The 15th and 21st Panzer Divisions deployed south of Tobruk and Gambut. Rommel placed the Afrika Division, though still not fully equipped, and four Italian infantry divisions around Tobruk. In all, he had at his command 414 German tanks, 154 Italian tanks, and 119,000 men. In addition, the Axis alliance in Cyrenaica had 320 serviceable aircraft, and another 750 were in reserve in Tripolitania, Italy, Greece, and Crete.

Rommel set November 21 as D-day for the attack on Tobruk, ignoring urgings of caution from General Bastico. The commander in chief was

A German staff car *(above)* pulls up before the fort at Capuzzo, which displays Italian and German flags after its recapture from the British. During 1941 and 1942, the outpost changed hands at least five times.

In July of 1941, Major General Walther Neumann-Silkow *(far right)* presents the Knight's Cross to an officer in his 15th Panzer. A British officer found this picture on the film in a German camera he had confiscated.

worried that the British would launch a major attack at the same time and catch the German and Italian forces off balance. But Rommel was adamant. He attributed Bastico's concern to "excessive Latin nervousness" and insisted that a postponement would only worsen his supply problems, creating an even greater imbalance between the Axis forces and the British. He ordered his staff to appear upbeat and to reassure the Italians that there was nothing to worry about. One officer characterized his commander's fixation on Tobruk as an "obsession."

On November 14, Rommel flew to Rome to press his case. Ironically, he had little trouble convincing the Italians. Field Marshal Ugo Cavallero, chief of staff of the Italian armed forces, distrusted Bastico and accepted Rommel's assurances that the British were too worried about having their line of retreat severed to launch a major offensive. The Germans were less convinced. When his lobbying seemed to be going nowhere, Rommel exploded. He accused the German liaison officer of being a coward and a "friend of the Italians." In a fury, he grabbed the telephone and called General Alfred Jodl, the Wehrmacht's chief of operations. "I hear that you wish me to give up the attack on Tobruk," he shouted. "I am completely disgusted." When Jodl demanded confirmation that there was no danger of a British attack, Rommel responded, "I give you my personal guarantee!"

Having won his argument, Rommel lingered a few extra days to celebrate

Operation Crusader's Flawed First Stages

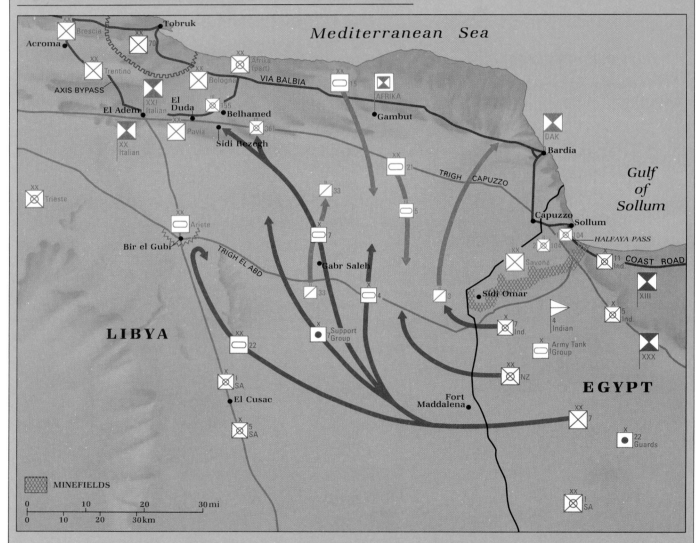

This map positions Axis troops and the attacking British Eighth Army as Crusader began. Crossing the border near Maddalena, the XXX Corps advanced to Gabr Saleh, where Cunningham planned to fight the 21st and 15th Panzer. After the German armor had been defeated, the Tobruk garrison was to break out while the XIII Corps attacked Rommel's Sollum-Sidi Omar defenses. When Rommel failed to react as expected, the British split their armored brigades: The 4th remained at Gabr Saleh, the 22d headed toward Bir el Gubi, and the 7th advanced toward Sidi Rezegh while the Support Group moved in between. The dispersal allowed Rommel to attack each separately.

his fiftieth birthday with his wife. He would soon discover that Bastico had been right. Rommel's carefully planned attack on Tobruk would not take place, because the enemy would beat him to the punch.

During the four and a half months following Battleaxe, General Auchinleck, like Rommel, had been constrained by various strategic and logistical considerations. As a result of the evacuation of British forces from Greece and Crete, he actually had more troops under his command than Wavell had had in the spring, but he was determined not to repeat Wavell's mistakes and send the men into battle before they were properly trained and equipped. Auchinleck was also reluctant to begin an offensive while Hitler's invasion of Russia held open the possibility of a German drive southward into the Middle East.

By November, the German offensive in Russia had come to a halt and Auchinleck had reorganized and reequipped his army. Compared with Rommel, he enjoyed an abundance of matériel. Thanks to the Royal Navy and the United States, which—though still at peace—had begun sending shipments of tanks and other vehicles through the Red Sea during the summer, he had a generous supply of new weapons. In all, Auchinleck received 300 Cruiser tanks, 300 American-made Stuart light tanks, 170 Matildas, 34,000 trucks, 600 field guns, 240 antiaircraft guns, 200 antitank guns, and 900 mortars. Because of a shortage of repair shops and skilled mechanics, he would have preferred building up larger reserves, especially in armor, but the quantity was sufficient. In addition, New Zealand engineers had extended the railway tracks from Alexandria to Misheifa, thirty miles south of Sidi Barrani. The pipeline for Auchinleck's water supply now stretched an extra 160 miles to the Misheifa railhead (although the troops were still limited to three quarts per man per day for all purposes).

The Allied offensive, called Operation Crusader, would be carried out by the Eighth Army, under the command of Lieut. General Sir Alan Cunningham. The Eighth Army boasted 118,000 men and more than 700 tanks. It had two sections: XXX Corps, led by Lieut. General C. W. M. Norrie, and XIII Corps, under Lieut. General Alfred Godwin-Austen. The XXX Corps consisted of the 7th Armored Division, with the 4th Armored Brigade attached, the South African 1st Infantry Division, and the 22d Guards Brigade. The XIII Corps included the New Zealand 2d and Indian 4th Divisions, backed by the 1st Army Tank Brigade. Air support would come from more than 600 planes of all types, flying out of Egypt and Malta.

Auchinleck's plan had a strong academic flavor. The main attack force, the armored units of the XXX Corps, would cross the Egyptian border near Maddalena, a village thirty-five miles south of the Germans' Sollum-Sidi

Omar defense line, and drive northwest in a great curve to a locality called Gabr Saleh, where Auchinleck hoped to compel Rommel's armor to fight. After defeating the Afrikakorps, the XXX Corps would advance to the high ground around Sidi Rezegh and link up with a breakout by the Tobruk garrison. At the same time, the XIII Corps infantry, on the northern flank of the XXX Corps, would advance to the Sollum-Sidi Omar defenses and "do the absolute minimum" until the XXX Corps had destroyed the two panzer divisions. The plan was predicated on the assumption that Rommel would follow the British script and send the Afrikakorps to do battle on the ground that the XXX Corps chose—Gabr Saleh. Yet there would be no compelling reason for the German commander to do so.

If the plan for Crusader was textbookish, the one the British attempted just five hours before the approach march to Gabr Saleh smacked of adventure fiction. On the night of November 17, a commando force attempted to eliminate Rommel and his staff in one bold strike. Put ashore from submarines, the commandos, operating on information provided by British intelligence and Arab collaborators, made their way to Beda Littoria and burst into what they thought was Rommel's headquarters. As it happened, not only did they have the wrong house, but Rommel was still in Italy. The commandos killed four Germans, including members of Rommel's quartermaster staff, before they were killed or captured themselves.

The commandos' near miss did not shake Rommel. He viewed it as an isolated incident and not the prelude to a major attack. But several of his commanders had been expecting at least a limited enemy offensive for some time. The two reconnaissance units in the desert had been instructed to transmit the code words *high water* if they saw evidence of a minor attack and the word *deluge* if they sensed a major attack. The words could not have been chosen better. On November 17, the day before the British offensive and the same day as the attempt on Rommel's life, a rainstorm of unprecedented intensity struck the Axis-occupied section of Cyrenaica. The spectacular storm touched off flash floods in the wadis, wiping out bridges, engulfing equipment, and drowning several soldiers. Worst for the Germans, the deluge turned their airfields to quagmires, making takeoffs and landings impossible. All reconnaissance flights were halted. As a result, several newly established supply dumps in the desert that would have revealed British intentions went unnoticed.

Nor was any information gleaned from the usually reliable wireless intercept service. Two days prior to the start of the battle, the British stopped all radio traffic. Although the silence was itself an indication that something was up, the Axis command was deprived of the kinds of specific information that had been so useful before and during Battleaxe.

Wading through ankle-deep water, German soldiers salvage what they can from their flooded campsite on the morning of November 19, 1941. The unexpected deluge washed out all Axis reconnaissance flights, ruining Rommel's last chance to forestall Operation Crusader.

During the afternoon of November 18, General Crüwell and his senior Afrikakorps commanders became alarmed at reports of scattered enemy sightings by the reconnaissance units. Crüwell ordered the 15th Panzer Division to move inland to face a potential assault, and at ten o'clock he went to Rommel's headquarters at Gambut to inform him. Rommel insisted that the British meant "only to harass us" and scoffed, "We must not lose our nerve." Despite Rommel's disapproval, Crüwell did not countermand his order. It was fortunate for Rommel that he did not. Panzergruppe Afrika and the British Eighth Army were about to lock horns in what would be recorded in the annals of war as one of the great armored clashes.

It would be a contest of constant maneuver by two motorized armies over swaths of desolate territory between Tobruk and the Egyptian-Libyan border. "Never has a battle been fought at such an extreme pace and with such bewildering vicissitudes of fortune," Major Friedrich von Mellenthin, Rommel's intelligence officer, would write. "More than a thousand tanks, supported by large numbers of aircraft and guns, were committed to a whirlwind battle fought on ground that allowed complete freedom of maneuver, and were handled by commanders who were prepared to throw in their last reserves to achieve victory. The situation changed so rapidly that it was difficult to keep track of the movements of one's own troops, let alone those of the enemy." Yet Crusader would begin quietly.

On November 18, the XXX Corps executed its approach march to Gabr Saleh, almost fifty miles southeast of Tobruk, as planned. The initiative was in British hands, but Cunningham and his commanders were puzzled by Rommel's lack of response. The next morning, Major General W. H. E. Gott split his 7th Armored Division and made a three-column reconnaissance.

On the left, the 22d Armored Brigade, equipped with new Crusader tanks, headed for Bir el Gubi. On the right, the 7th Armored Brigade advanced northwest toward Sidi Rezegh, while the Support Group moved between the two brigades, ready to help either one. Only the 4th Armored Brigade remained at Gabr Saleh to guard the division's right flank.

On November 19, the 22d Armored encountered a company of Italian tanks south of Bir el Gubi. Without Cunningham's knowledge, General Gott ordered an attack, which one officer described as the "nearest thing to a cavalry charge with tanks seen during the war." The British soon had the small Italian force on the run. But the impetuous charge led the swift Crusader tanks straight to the Ariete Division's entrenched positions. Attacking despite weak artillery support, the 22d Armored lost 25 of its 136 tanks before breaking off the action. This initial clash would play a large role in shaping future British actions; because the 22d Armored was embroiled in a pitched battle on the extreme left, Cunningham would have trouble concentrating his tanks.

Meanwhile, the 7th Armored Brigade, led by Brigadier G. M. O. Davy, was ordered to seize a position on the edge of the escarpment rising from the coastal plain. This was Sidi Rezegh, site of an old Arab tomb on a bleak stretch of rocky ground. Over the next two weeks, Sidi Rezegh would be the scene of two bloody battles, because it was a prize greater than it seemed. It possessed an airstrip, and the surrounding high ground overlooked the perimeter of the Tobruk defenses, ten miles to the northwest. Sidi Rezegh was even closer to the new bypass road and the Trigh Capuzzo, a desert track along which Axis supplies moved to Bardia, Sollum, and the frontier defensive lines. Davy's forces quickly took the airfield, capturing nineteen Italian planes and threatening the Afrika Division, which was deployed on the high ground north of the airfield.

Back at Gabr Saleh, the 4th Armored, under Brigadier A. H. Gatehouse, was enjoying the fine autumn weather. "The air was crisp," a soldier recalled, "and there were occasional patches of sunshine." The crews of 3d Royal Tanks, driving fast, lightweight Stuarts, had chased the German 3d Reconnaissance Detachment more than twenty miles north, beyond the Trigh Capuzzo. The Stuarts were dangerously near the limit of their operating radius when they were recalled to Gabr Saleh: The remainder of their brigade had come under heavy attack by a German battle group.

Reports of the 7th Armored Division's activity had convinced Generals Crüwell and Ravenstein that a major British offensive was indeed developing. With Rommel's approval, Crüwell dispatched from the 21st Panzer a force consisting of 120 tanks, twelve field guns, and four 88-mm guns, to support the reconnaissance units. These reinforcements collided head-on

A lone German soldier stands before freshly filled graves near the tomb of a Muslim prophet at Sidi Rezegh, the scene of bloody fighting southeast of Tobruk. "Apart from the little white-domed building, there was nothing to justify its having a name," an officer recalled. "We never thought it would remain in our memories forever."

with Gatehouse's 4th Armored. In a violent battle of equal numbers of tanks, the Germans got much the better of it, putting twenty-three Stuarts out of action and losing only a few panzers.

That evening, Rommel was still thinking about Tobruk. The day's fighting had convinced him that the British thrust was meant only to distract him from attacking the besieged city, and he ordered Crüwell to destroy the enemy forces before they could intervene. Crüwell instructed the 15th Panzer to move east while the 21st Panzer proceeded to Sidi Omar to cut off the British line of retreat.

So far, the battle had not gone well for Cunningham. His tanks and mobile guns were scattered about the desert. A New Zealand officer wrote, "It was not a good beginning to a battle whose aim was the total destruction of enemy armor." But Rommel's forces were also dispersed. The next day, November 20, each side would get a clearer picture of the other's intentions. Crüwell was operating on the assumption that the enemy was split into three groups—the force at Gabr Saleh, another at Sidi Rezegh, and a third that had chased the 3d Reconnaissance Detachment across the Trigh Capuzzo. He decided that, rather than fight a series of small clashes, he should concentrate his panzers and destroy the enemy columns one by one. The first encounter would take place at Gabr Saleh.

Now it was the British turn to benefit from radio intercepts. Cunningham's monitors overheard Crüwell's plans and alerted General Norrie, commander of the XXX Corps. Norrie hastily recalled the 22d Armored from Bir el Gubi, sending the South African 1st Division to keep the Italians there occupied. Confident that the armored battle he desired was about to

happen, Norrie approved a sortie by the Tobruk garrison for the next day.

The opening clash at Gabr Saleh, however, was only a prelude. The 21st Panzer had run out of gasoline on its drive east to Sidi Omar and arrived too late after an all-night forced march. On the British side, the 22d Armored also arrived from Bir el Gubi too late to be effective. The 15th Panzer, with 135 tanks, drove the British south, destroying or damaging about two dozen tanks but gaining no major advantage.

That night, Rommel realized the danger facing his forces. Thinking that the 4th Armored Brigade had been disposed of, he decided to concentrate the Afrikakorps at Sidi Rezegh and eliminate the threat posed to his siege of Tobruk by the 7th Armored Brigade and the divisional Support Group. Assigning a rear guard to hold back the 4th and 22d Armored at Gabr Saleh, the 15th and 21st Panzer disengaged and raced northwest to begin three days of the hardest fighting yet in the desert war *(map, next page)*.

The next morning, November 21, the panzer divisions arrived at Sidi Rezegh just as the British 70th Division, led by Major General R. M. Scobie, launched a massive breakout from Tobruk. The sortie was to be coordinated with an attack by the 7th Armored and the Support Group. But Brigadier Davy's men would soon be fighting for their lives at Sidi Rezegh and unable to come to Scobie's aid. By afternoon, the 70th had broken through units of the Afrika and the Bologna Divisions, opened a salient nearly 4,000 yards deep, and captured more than 1,000 German and Italian troops. Rommel, who had arrived in the area to oversee the investment, reacted immediately. He took command of the 3d Reconnaissance Detachment, reinforced by 88-mm guns, and checked Scobie's breakout.

Meanwhile, in violent fighting at Sidi Rezegh, the guns of the 7th Armored's Support Group had prevented the Afrikakorps from seizing the airfield. But the two panzer divisions had almost wiped out the 7th Armored Division, which had joined the fray from Gabr Saleh.

By nightfall, the Afrikakorps occupied a central position between the Support Group, what remained of the 7th Armored Brigade, and the battered 4th and 22d Armored Brigades. A British officer described the alignment of opposing armies: "Over the twenty or so miles of country from the front of the Tobruk sortie to the open desert southeast of Sidi Rezegh airfield, the forces of both sides were sandwiched like the layers of a Neapolitan ice." A German called it a "truly peculiar situation. Not only did the German-Italian forces occupying the line of investment find themselves between two fires, but the British forces on Sidi Rezegh were threatened by the Afrikakorps in the rear, while the Afrikakorps had also to hold off strong enemy attacks against its flank and rear."

Because supplies and ammunition were running low, Crüwell decided

An Impulsive Stab toward Egypt

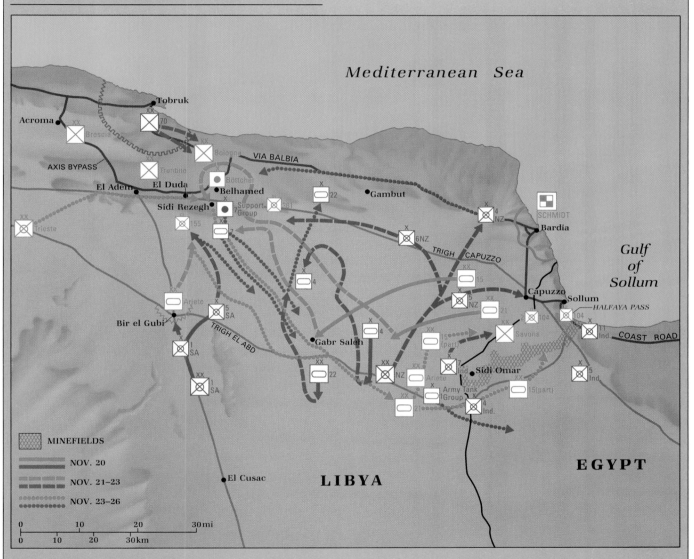

Mediterranean Sea

Tobruk

Acroma

AXIS BYPASS

Brescia

Bologna

VIA BALBIA

Trentino

El Adem

El Duda

Belhamed

Böttcher

Gambut

Sidi Rezegh

Support Group

SCHMIDT

Bardia

Trieste

Gulf of Sollum

TRIGH CAPUZZO

Capuzzo

Sollum

HALFAYA PASS

Bir el Gubi

Ariete

COAST ROAD

TRIGH EL ABD

Gabr Saleh

Sidi Omar

Army Tank Group

Savona

MINEFIELDS

NOV. 20

NOV. 21–23

NOV. 23–26

0   10   20   30 mi

0   10   20   30 km

El Cusac

LIBYA

EGYPT

This map traces the whirlwind movements of Axis armor and British forces November 19-26, as the fighting careened between Tobruk and the Egyptian border. On November 20, Rommel, thinking that his 15th Panzer had disposed of the British 4th Armored Brigade at Gabr Saleh, sent the 15th and 21st Panzer Divisions to Sidi Rezegh. There, the Germans smashed the 7th Armored Division and foiled a breakout by the Tobruk garrison. But instead of finishing off the enemy, Rommel, hoping to achieve total victory, sent his armor to the Egyptian frontier to cut off British supplies. The gamble failed, because the New Zealand 2d Division had bypassed Axis border defenses and was threatening Tobruk. On November 26, the New Zealanders opened a corridor into the town, forcing the Afrikakorps to return for a showdown.

75

to extricate the Afrikakorps from the "sandwich" at Sidi Rezegh and move roughly northward during the night to regroup. Leaving rear guards south of the airfield, the 15th Panzer moved south of Gambut while the 21st Panzer headed toward Belhamed, eighteen miles away. Crüwell's decision to split the Afrikakorps enabled the 7th Armored Division to reconcentrate its brigades, which together still possessed 200 serviceable tanks.

Cunningham had given the go-ahead for the XIII Corps to attack Rommel's frontier line. While the tank battle raged at Sidi Rezegh, the New Zealand 2d Division, bypassing Halfaya Pass, reached the Bardia-Sollum area, the Trigh Capuzzo, and Sidi Azeiz. On November 22, the division seized Capuzzo and Musaid, blocked the coast road between Bardia and Tobruk, and cut all German and Italian telegraph and telephone lines to the area. Thinking that he had neutralized the Afrikakorps, Cunningham ordered the New Zealanders to advance toward Tobruk. But Rommel would turn the tables again. At noon that day, he ordered a counterattack at Sidi Rezegh. The infantry and most of the artillery of the 21st Panzer were to attack the escarpment from the north, while its 5th Panzer Regiment, after detouring around the escarpment, attacked from the west. Both units would be supported by the Panzergruppe's heavy artillery.

That afternoon, the German armor caught the British by surprise. The 88-mm and antitank guns on the high ground around the airfield devastated the 22d Armored, forcing it to withdraw with only thirty-four of its seventy-nine tanks. The 7th Armored was in even worse shape, reduced to a mere ten tanks. Meanwhile, the 15th Panzer was coming into action from the west on the opposite flank. By chance, the Germans' path to the battlefield took them directly through the area where the 4th Armored was camped. Shortly after sunset, the panzers smashed into the brigade's headquarters, capturing 267 men and 50 tanks.

Rommel sensed the kill. He telegraphed Mussolini asking for permission to unite all the Axis forces under a single command. The Italian dictator responded swiftly, placing General Gambara's XX Corps (the Ariete Armored and the Trieste Motorized Divisions) under Rommel. As Colonel Bayerlein recalled, "Orders for 23 November were to destroy the enemy's main striking force by a concentric attack of all German-Italian mobile forces." Crüwell ordered the 15th Panzer and one regiment from the 21st Panzer to join forces with the Ariete Division, advancing from Bir el Gubi. Their mission was to attack the rest of the enemy armor thought to be lying on the desert plateau south of Sidi Rezegh and drive it against the infantry and artillery of the 21st Panzer, which held the escarpment at the airfield.

As Crüwell was organizing Rommel's surprise, however, he was nearly surprised himself. The advance of the New Zealanders from the east had gone unnoticed, and shortly after dawn a unit of the New Zealand 6th Brigade happened upon Crüwell's headquarters at Gasr el Arid. Crüwell had already departed, but his entire staff was captured. Bayerlein wrote later that "General Crüwell and I escaped this fate by a hairsbreadth."

Despite the close call, Crüwell continued his attempt at envelopment. As the combined German and Italian force moved north into the British rear, it encountered a screen of artillery and antitank guns deployed by the South Africans between Bir el Haiad and Sidi Muftah. The panzers, followed by the infantry in trucks, formed up in long lines and charged. "Guns of all kinds and sizes laid a curtain of fire, and there seemed almost no hope of making any progress in the face of this fire-spewing barrier," Bayerlein recalled. "Tank after tank split open in the hail of shells. Our entire artillery had to be thrown in to silence the enemy guns, one by one. However, by late afternoon we had managed to punch a few holes in the front. The tank

Wrecked vehicles, including the demolished reconnaissance car in the foreground, clutter the desert after a clash between British and German armor. By November 30, Operation Crusader had become a battle of attrition; although the Axis forces lost fewer men and less matériel, they were worse off than the British because their losses could not be replaced.

attack moved forward again, and tank duels of tremendous intensity developed deep in the battlefield."

As the melee ranged across the plain, someone tapped on the hatch of Crüwell's armored command vehicle, which had been captured from the British. The Afrikakorps's commander flipped it open and found himself face to face with a British soldier, inside a ring of British tanks. The tanks, it turned out, were out of ammunition and under fire from a German gun. Equally astonished, the British restarted their vehicles, and everyone fled.

Fighting raged into the night. "The wide plain south of Sidi Rezegh was now a sea of dust, haze, and smoke," Bayerlein wrote. "Twilight came, but the battle was still not over. Hundreds of burning vehicles, tanks, and guns lit up the field." In some British units, only a handful of guns and troops remained. "Firing at point-blank range, with apparently no hope of survival, these indomitable men still fought their guns," a British officer recalled. "In the light of burning vehicles and dumps, our guns slipped out of action, leaving the field to a relentlessly advancing enemy, who loomed in large, fantastic shapes out of the shadows in the glare of the bursting shells."

The casualties were horrendous. The South African 5th Brigade, which had absorbed the brunt of Crüwell's attack, ceased to exist as a fighting force. It had lost almost all its artillery and antitank guns, along with 224 men killed, 379 wounded, and 2,791 captured. And of the 150 German panzers engaged, 70 had been put out of action. Most of the officers and noncoms of the motorized infantry had been killed or wounded. Appalled by the Afrikakorps's losses, Major Mellenthin sarcastically described Crüwell's attack as an "innovation in tactics that proved a costly experiment." But Bayerlein exulted at "the elimination of the direct threat to the Tobruk front, the destruction of a large part of the enemy armor, and the damage to enemy morale caused by the complete ruination of his plans."

The clash at Sidi Rezegh may have seemed decisive, but the battle was far from over. General Norrie, commander of the XXX Corps, decided to withdraw what remained of his forces southward to the Gabr Saleh area. Two-thirds of his tanks had been lost. Half of the South African division remained in reserve; the remnants of the 7th Armored Division, consisting of some forty tanks that had managed to slip away south of Bir el Gubi, were still dangerous; and the New Zealanders of the XIII Corps threatened Tobruk from the east. Even before learning the details of how badly the enemy had been smashed at Sidi Rezegh, Rommel, following his instinct for surprise, had decided to exploit the confusion in the British camp. The lopsided victory only confirmed the decision.

Instead of mopping up the British formations, as Crüwell advised, Rommel proposed to ignore them and, as he had done in June, strike into their

Victory and a Prudent Retreat

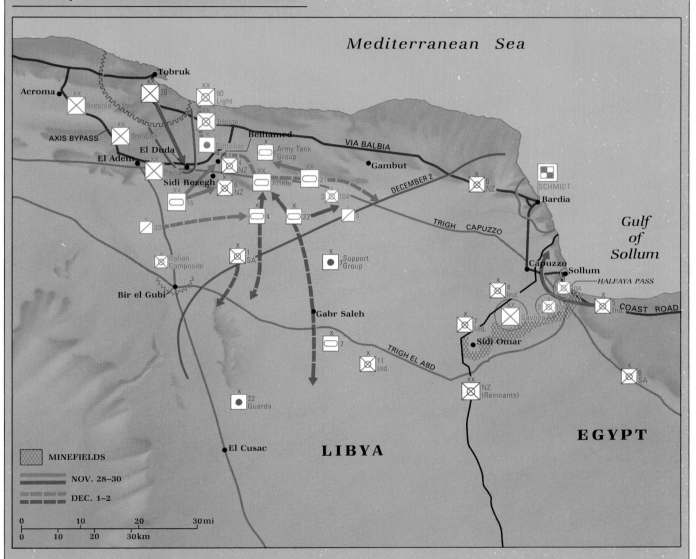

On December 1, Erwin Rommel launched an attack that was aimed at destroying the New Zealand 2d at Belhamed, El Duda, and Sidi Rezegh. The 15th Panzer attacked from the west, the 21st Panzer from the east, the 90th Light Division from the north, and the Ariete Division from the south. The result was a crushing victory, but the Axis forces were too depleted to press their advantage. After detachments of the Afrikakorps tried in vain to resupply the Bardia garrison, which was being attacked by units of the British XXX Corps, Rommel learned that the enemy was regrouping at Bir el Gubi and threatening his rear. On December 5, he abandoned the investment of Tobruk and began a fighting retreat to the Gazala Line, fifty miles to the west.

rear. "The greater part of the force aimed at Tobruk has been destroyed," he told Crüwell. "Now we will turn east and go for the New Zealanders and Indians before they are able to join up with the remains of their main force for a combined attack on Tobruk. Speed is vital; we must make the most of the shock effect of the enemy's defeat and push forward as fast as we can with our entire force to Sidi Omar." His plan was to surround and destroy the British forces on the Egyptian frontier with one stroke.

Leaving a holding force in the Sidi Rezegh-Tobruk area, Rommel placed Lieut. Colonel Siegfried Westphal, his chief of operations, in command at Panzergruppe headquarters at El Adem and ordered the two panzer divisions and the Ariete Division eastward, toward the Sollum front. On the morning of November 24, Rommel rode at the head of the 21st Panzer as German armor began what Bayerlein described as a "wild drive in complete disregard of the British threat to their flanks." Late that afternoon, Rommel reached the wire that marked the frontier, and the Afrikakorps stretched

Rommel's armored command
vehicle, a captured British
Dorchester, was called a Mammoth by the Germans be-
cause of its great size. The
nickname he gave it, Moritz, after
a character in a German chil-
dren's story, was painted on
the front and is visible beneath
the camouflage netting.

out behind him over forty miles of desert. His bold move threw the XXX Corps into confusion. "Although this advance happened to pass out of snapping distance of most of the 7th Armored Division's remaining teeth, it swept before it many units and stragglers," a British officer wrote. "The advanced and rear headquarters of XXX Corps were caught up in the flurry. Some lorries had never traveled so fast."

On the evening of November 24, on the Egyptian side of the frontier, the vehicle carrying Rommel and Gause, his chief of staff, broke down. As night was falling, the marooned commander was discovered by Crüwell, who was somewhat lost himself. For hours, Crüwell's armored command vehicle, with most of the senior officers of the Afrikakorps on board and Rommel at the wheel, lumbered along the wire barrier, looking for a way to get back through. All around them, wrote Bayerlein, "Indian dispatch riders buzzed to and fro past the Mammoth, British tanks moved forward, and American-built trucks ground their way through the desert."

While the Germans indulged in misadventure, Cunningham despaired. Because his main armor had been shattered and Rommel was far to his rear, he saw no alternative to retreat. Unlike Wavell, however, Auchinleck was having none of that. He relieved Cunningham of command, replacing him with Major General Neil Ritchie, and took charge of the fighting.

Rommel's decision to head east had been made too hastily and with a poor understanding of the enemy's dispositions. Although the advance had caused a stampede of British service troops, some of the German units came under sharp attack. "It soon became apparent that the enemy was everywhere and still far stronger than might have been expected," wrote Bayerlein. While half of the 21st Panzer wandered about south of Halfaya Pass against no opposition, its 5th Panzer Regiment was losing half its strength in vain attacks at Sidi Omar. The men of the Afrikakorps were growing increasingly weary and short of food, water, and fuel. The brilliant counterstroke, as one officer put it, had turned into an "evil dream." And to make matters worse, the New Zealand 2d Division, which Rommel thought was still at the Sollum front, was closing in on Tobruk.

On November 25, the New Zealanders captured the Sidi Rezegh airfield. The following day, the Tobruk garrison broke through the Axis investment and linked up with New Zealanders on the escarpment at El Duda. Colonel Westphal, who had expected Rommel to return the evening of November 24 or the next morning at the latest, tried desperately to contact his superior. But the wireless radio truck accompanying Rommel had been left behind, putting him completely out of touch with his operations staff. As the situation south of Tobruk worsened, Westphal took matters into his own hands: He recalled the 21st Panzer to Sidi Rezegh.

When Rommel finally started back toward Tobruk with the Afrikakorps, elements of the restored 7th Armored Division attacked his flank from the south, but the 15th and 21st Panzer were only slightly deflected. They prepared to attack the New Zealanders outside the still partially besieged city. On November 29, the 21st Panzer suffered a great blow when the New Zealanders captured its commander, General Johann von Ravenstein, along with all his maps and documents. Even with that advantage, however, the British could not stop the Germans.

By December 1, Rommel's forces had surrounded the New Zealand 2d Division. The attack began at dawn. A portion of the New Zealanders broke out, but about 1,000 men were captured, along with twenty-six guns. The siege had been restored. Rommel telegraphed the news to Hitler: "In the uninterrupted fighting of 18 November to 1 December, 814 enemy tanks and scout cars were destroyed and 127 aircraft shot down. The number of prisoners exceeds 9,000, including three generals."

Captured German and Italian troops who garrisoned Halfaya Pass wait to be trucked to prison camps. Before the men surrendered, their typical daily ration had been reduced to twenty grams of bread, a handful of rice, a spoonful of currants, and a few ounces of water.

Nonetheless, the Afrikakorps could not keep going much longer. While replacement tanks flowed to the British side of the front, Rommel's reserves were exhausted. "On paper, we seemed to have won the Crusader battle," Major Mellenthin later declared, "but the price paid was too heavy. The Panzergruppe had been worn down, and it soon became clear that only one course remained—a general retreat from Cyrenaica."

Rommel refused to accept such a verdict. On December 3, he ordered units from the Afrikakorps eastward to resupply the fortress at Bardia. He still hoped to drive the enemy there into the minefields along his defensive positions. But the German detachment was too weak to get through and returned almost at once to Sidi Rezegh.

The next day, December 4, when reports of massing British troops near Bir el Gubi reached Rommel, he ordered the Afrikakorps and General Gambara's Ariete and Trieste Divisions to attack before the enemy could concentrate. During the night, the panzers moved to an assembly area at

Fulfilling his surrender terms, Major Wilhelm Bach *(center)* explains to British combat engineers where Axis land mines are planted at Halfaya Pass. For his stubborn resistance, Britons dubbed the German minister the Pastor of Hellfire Pass.

El Adem. When the Italians failed to appear, the Germans set out for Bir el Gubi alone to face the 22d Guards Brigade, the Indian 11th Brigade, and elements of the refitted 7th Armored Division.

Although the beleaguered Afrikakorps fought the British to a standstill at Bir el Gubi, the Axis siege forces at Tobruk were unable to contain another breakout. On December 5, the British 70th Division seized the vital El Duda-Belhamed heights. That same day, an officer from the Italian high command brought Rommel more bad news: His Panzergruppe could expect no reinforcements before January. Yet Rommel still thought he could turn the tide. He now ordered a withdrawal from the eastern part of the Tobruk front and an all-out attack by his panzers against the British at Bir el Gubi. Once more, however, the Afrikakorps found itself alone. During the fighting, Crüwell repeatedly radioed Rommel, asking angrily, "Where is Gambara?" According to Bayerlein, the Italian commanders responded that their troops were "exhausted and no longer fit for action." After two more days of bitter fighting, Rommel decided to pull back from the Tobruk area to a defensive line that the Italians had built south of Gazala, forty miles away. "It was," wrote Bayerlein, "a painful decision." During the night of December 7, the Afrikakorps broke away from the enemy and headed west.

By December 12, all of Rommel's forces had reached the Gazala Line. The following day, the British attacked. Because the enemy threatened to outflank him by coming up behind the Gazala Line and taking Mechili, Rommel ordered a complete withdrawal.

Rommel's decision provoked a crisis in the Axis high command. On December 16, he began a series of meetings at Gazala with his superiors, General Bastico and Field Marshal Albert Kesselring, the Wehrmacht commander in chief, South, and General Cavallero, the Italian chief of staff, who had flown in from Rome. Abandoning Cyrenaica would be a terrible blow to Mussolini's prestige, and the order to retreat hit the Italians, recalled a German officer, like a lightning bolt. When Bastico demanded that the order be rescinded, Rommel angrily asked how he proposed to handle the situation. Bastico replied, "As commander in chief, it is not my business."

In the end, Rommel had his way. The fighting retreat continued until early in January 1942, when Rommel reached Mersa Brega and El Agheila—and fresh troops, tanks, and stores. Far to the east, the 8,800-man German-Italian garrison at Bardia fell, followed by the Sollum garrison, with 6,300 troops. Yet the fight was not over. Major Bach and his men maintained their iron grip on Halfaya Pass, pinning down a British division and blocking the shortest supply route from Egypt. Not until January 17 did the former pastor bow to the inevitable and surrender his isolated command, ending the ten-month struggle for Tobruk where it had begun. ✚

The Long Reach of the Lethal 88

"The struggle in the desert is best compared to a battle at sea," Erwin Rommel told a group of his officers in Libya as they braced for a British offensive. "Whoever has the weapons with the greatest range has the longest arm." Rommel conceded that the British, who had recently been reinforced with hundreds of tanks, would enjoy unprecedented mobility in the coming fight. Nonetheless, he insisted "the longest arm has the advantage. We have it—the 88-mm gun."

Rommel's faith in this versatile artillery piece *(right)* was fully warranted. Krupp, the vaunted armaments firm, had developed the gun as an antiaircraft weapon during the late 1920s in secret defiance of the Versailles treaty. Commonly called the 88, for the diameter of its muzzle in millimeters, the gun was first deployed during the Spanish Civil War, where German commanders lowered its barrel to fire on Russian tanks, with devastating results. The 88's next test in that role came during the German drive on Dunkirk in May of 1940, when the British struck back at Rommel's 7th Panzer Division with heavily armored tanks that were invulnerable to the standard German 37-mm antitank gun. Called in to meet the threat, the 88s stymied the assault—one battery alone knocked out nine of the British tanks. Henceforth, the weapon would loom large in Rommel's plans.

Because they were technically antiaircraft guns, all 88-mm batteries assigned to the Afrikakorps came under the aegis of the Luftwaffe, which trained the crews and awarded veterans of successful ground actions the same decoration given those who shot down enemy planes—a pin that showed the gun barrel elevated for antiaircraft duty *(inset)*. In the field, however, the batteries were at Rommel's disposal, and his crafty use of the 88 against armor made it the bane of his foe's existence. One British officer who was taken prisoner after an 88 crippled his tank summed up the frustration of those who endured its fire: "That's not fair, to use an antiaircraft gun against a tank!"

Hurrying into action near Tobruk in May 1941, crewmen

prepare an 88-mm gun for firing. The eight white rings around the barrel signal the number of tanks the gun has destroyed.

A Flak Gun Adapted to Stop Tanks

The 88 owed much of its success against tanks to features devised for its antiaircraft role. Krupp designers foresaw that, as bombers flew faster and higher, a flak crew would have to unleash a flurry of shots to have any chance of downing its target. So they equipped the 88 with a spring mechanism that opened the breech and ejected the casing as the gun recoiled, then rammed a fresh shell home; the man feeding the gun simply laid the ammunition in the loading cradle. Useful when the barrel was elevated, the self-loader proved a liability when the gun was fired horizontally. A good crew could fire faster without it. Consequently, it was generally removed in antitank warfare.

Firing up to twenty rounds a minute with each of its four guns, a battery could cope with dozens of tanks at a time; a lone 88 battery once held off fifty tanks. Similarly, the range of the 88—designed to propel flak 26,000 feet upward—conferred a premium against armor. Gunners could hit tanks more than two miles away, although the Germans preferred to wait until the target was within a thousand yards. At that distance, the shell arrived in a little over one second and could pierce the heaviest British armor.

To haul the gun and its crew, the Germans relied on a half-track that made the 88 seem small by comparison (right). Indeed, at five and a half tons, the gun was not the behemoth some imagined it to be. A British tank commander who had tangled with an 88 remarked glumly, "It doesn't look like much, but nothing can be done against it."

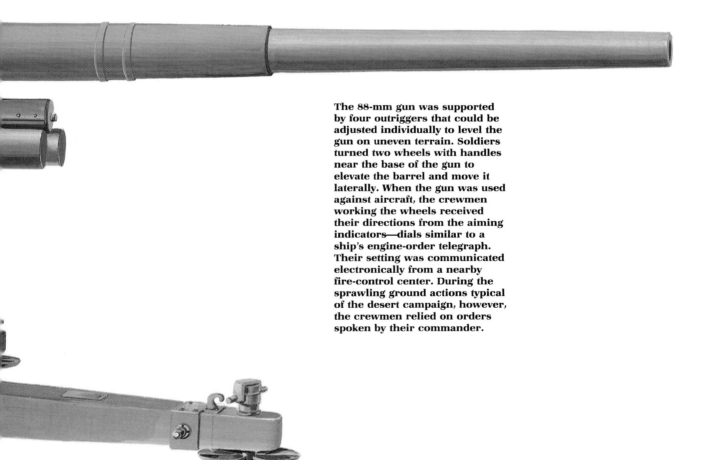

The 88-mm gun was supported by four outriggers that could be adjusted individually to level the gun on uneven terrain. Soldiers turned two wheels with handles near the base of the gun to elevate the barrel and move it laterally. When the gun was used against aircraft, the crewmen working the wheels received their directions from the aiming indicators—dials similar to a ship's engine-order telegraph. Their setting was communicated electronically from a nearby fire-control center. During the sprawling ground actions typical of the desert campaign, however, the crewmen relied on orders spoken by their commander.

An 88-mm gun crew removes shells from a wicker crate near their gun, which is partially protected by a wall of sandbags.

Digging In to Deliver a Nasty Surprise

When action was imminent, the crew of an 88-mm gun would simply emplace the weapon, erect a ring of sandbags *(above)*, and prepare to fire. But whenever time permitted, the crew would dig in so that the barrel, when level, was just above the surface of the ground *(above, right)*. Such concealment took advantage of the desert haze, which cloaked from view objects that were near the ground, enabling the gun to remain undetected as tanks approached. Then the powerful 88, which could be aimed with optical sights much like a rifle, would open fire at easy range.

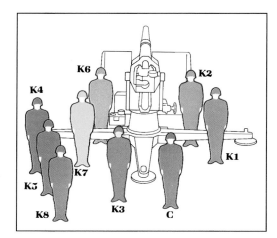

The typical 88 crew consisted of a commander and a squad of eight; each *Kanonier*, or gunner, was assigned a number and deployed as shown at left. The commander (C)—after gauging the range with the optical sights or relying on a nearby observer—shouted orders to the gunners (K1 and K2) operating the elevation and traverse wheels. K6 adjusted a device that set the shells' fuses to explode at a prescribed distance or upon impact, K7 inserted each shell's nose into the fuse-setting device, and K3 hefted the twenty-five-pound projectile into the breech, closed it, and fired the gun on command. The remaining crewmen (K4, K5, and K8) passed shells forward to K7. When an 88 was facing only tanks, the crew could use armor-piercing rounds with fuses that exploded on impact.

Helmeted crew members stand by their gun in a well-excavated position. Such emplacements presented an obscure target at best and were almost invisible when the desert floor was shimmering under a high sun.

An observer uses a stereoscopic telescope to gauge the effect of shots fired by a nearby 88. The periscope-like device could also be used as a rough range finder.

Earning New Stripes at Halfaya Pass

The 88 came into its own as a tank killer during the British attack on Rommel's forces at Halfaya Pass in June 1941. Prior to the assault, rumors swept the German lines that the enemy was forming a huge armored force. "The Tommies have a new tank that antitank shells ricochet off of like peas," a sergeant said. After fending off heavily armored British Matildas in Belgium the year before, however, Rommel doubted anything the Allies sent his way could withstand the 88.

Having had plenty of time to dig in, Rommel's gun crews were ideally positioned to surprise the British tanks at short range. "Don't shoot under any circumstances" was the order of the hour as enemy armor neared the pass on June 15. "Let them come to you." The big tanks were so close when the 88s finally opened up that the thunder of the gun and the crash of the shell hitting its mark were compressed into one deafening sound. The encounter at Halfaya set the pattern for the fighting in the months ahead. Stung time and again by the 88, the British learned to fear Rommel's long arm more than any other weapon in his desert arsenal.

Observers *(below)* look out from their deep position as an 88, its barrel level for close-range firing, seeks a kill to add to the five it has already. The spectacle of smoke spewing from British armor that had run afoul of an 88 *(right)* became a recurring motif in the desert war. As the official British summary of the Halfaya debacle put it, "The 88-mm guns, well concealed, proved deadly to any tank."

Target: Tobruk

Erwin Rommel wrote to his wife, Lucie, on January 17, 1942, in circumstances that did not seem to justify the reassuring words he offered her. The exhausted commander of a beaten army, he had seen 33,000 of his troops taken prisoner in the past two months, including the capitulation that day of the garrison at Halfaya Pass, on the Egyptian frontier. Rommel was 350 miles west of Halfaya, marking time at the Libyan village of El Agheila, where the Afrikakorps had launched its costly campaign the previous March. Far from betraying any sense of despair, however, Rommel's letter home burst with optimism. "The situation is developing to our advantage," he wrote, "and I'm full of plans that I dare not say anything about around here. They'd think I was crazy. But I'm not. I simply see a bit farther than they do."

What only Rommel and a few of his senior staff officers saw was the opportunity to strike back at the British forces that were harrying them. German intelligence agents had eavesdropped on wireless reports sent to Washington by the American military attaché in Cairo, and Rommel knew from these intercepts that the British were vulnerable. The drive across the desert had overextended their supply lines, and the Luftwaffe's pounding of Benghazi prevented them from using that nearby port. In addition, Japan's entry into the war on December 7 had forced the British to divert planes, tanks, and two full infantry divisions from North Africa to Malaya and other threatened Asian colonies.

At the same time, Berlin was pumping new life into Rommel's command. Tanks, crews, and supplies reached Tripoli in increasing numbers, thanks to the protection provided by an expanded Mediterranean force of two dozen U-boats and by Field Marshal Albert Kesselring's air fleet, Luftflotte 2, which moved its headquarters to Sicily from the Russian front. In two months, the U-boats had sunk a carrier, a battleship, and a cruiser. Kesselring's II Air Corps flew cover for Axis convoys and, in Rommel's words, "knocked the stuffing" out of the British naval and air bases on Malta. The combined effort virtually eliminated Axis shipping losses, which in November had reached 77 percent. One convoy that docked at Tripoli on

An Italian soldier of the Afrika-korps gestures triumphantly as his Fiat armored car rolls into Tobruk in June 1942, capping a five-month-long offensive in which Rommel's army rebounded from defeat and drove the British forces from Libya.

January 5 delivered fifty-four tanks—a bonanza for Rommel's battered force, which had lost 90 percent of its armor in ten months of campaigning.

As the fresh men and machines reached El Agheila, Rommel's intelligence officers informed their chief that he actually enjoyed a temporary superiority over the enemy forces in his vicinity—hence the enthusiastic "Dear Lu" letter. Until Allied reinforcements came up, for example, he had a slight numerical edge over the 150 tanks in the British 1st Armored Division, which had just reached the front to relieve the so-called Desert Rats of the 7th Armored Division. "I feel I've got an attack coming on," Rommel confided to one of his staff officers. He decided to take the offensive on January 21, before the British could build up sufficient strength to regain the advantage—and push him even farther from Egypt.

Rommel wrapped this spoiling attack in the tightest security. He informed only a few key subordinates and failed to tell either his nominal Italian superiors or his actual bosses in Berlin. He fostered rumors that he

Spotted like a leopard in order to resemble the mottled desert terrain and elude detection from above, an Me 109 fighter prowls at low altitude in support of German ground forces. To confound enemy flak batteries, the underside of the plane was cleverly painted sky blue.

from Mussolini to remain on the defensive, he told Rommel, "Make it no more than a sortie and then come straight back." Rommel retorted that he intended to continue the offensive and that "nobody but the Führer" could change his mind. Rommel noted in his diary that his rebuttal had its intended effect: Cavallero "went off growling" and left him alone.

Operating for the moment without two of the Italian corps—which Cavallero held back temporarily out of spite—Rommel pushed ahead with his plan to destroy the retreating British tank force. He knew that the 1st Armored Division was vulnerable because of its inexperience. Unlike the Germans, who fed replacements into existing divisions in North Africa and thus perpetuated unit skills and pride, the British substituted entire raw units. In addition, Rommel retained the element of surprise: British commanders had underestimated his tank strength by half and refused to believe that his counterstroke was anything more than a reconnaissance in force. Yet he faced a daunting task in surrounding his prey—a maneuver that was particularly difficult in the Sahara, where there were few obstacles to pin an opponent against. As it turned out, a foul-up in the transmission of orders foiled Rommel's plans. German armor advancing from Antelat failed to occupy Saunnu after Group Marcks had moved south on January 23, leaving a gap that the British soon exploited. The Germans did make contact with elements of the 1st Armored Division and inflicted heavy losses, which Rommel at first interpreted as proof that the operation had succeeded. Not until late the following day did he realize that most of the British tanks had slipped away. As Rommel's intelligence chief, Major Friedrich von Mellenthin, remarked, the operation "proved yet again how difficult it is to encircle armored formations in the desert."

Rommel was not to be denied, however. On January 25, his panzers resumed the chase, roaring northward toward Msus. Repeatedly, they caught up with lagging British tank formations and hit them on the run. "At times, the pursuit attained a speed of fifteen miles per hour," Mellenthin wrote. "The British columns fled madly over the desert in one of the most extraordinary routs of the war." The 15th Panzer Division covered the fifty miles to Msus in less than four hours. It swept through several enemy supply columns and arrived at the airfield there in time to seize a dozen British aircraft on the ground, adding to the day's tally of 96 tanks, 38 guns, and 190 trucks captured or destroyed. "Now the tables are turned with a vengeance," Rommel exulted.

From Msus, Rommel was tempted to move northeastward by the inland route he had taken the previous spring to the old fort at Mechili. But his panzers lacked the fuel for a major push across nearly eighty-five miles of open desert, so he opted instead to recapture the port of Benghazi, seventy

miles to the northwest and accessible to German convoys. Late on January 27, he dispatched his panzers toward Mechili in a masterly feint. It fooled the British, who concentrated their armor at Mechili, leaving Benghazi uncovered. Then Rommel himself led Group Marcks toward the real objective, slogging through mountain passes and marshy wilderness, through a sandstorm and pouring rain. Twenty-four hours later, his column of trucks and armored cars reached Regima, an abandoned Turkish fortress sixteen miles east of Benghazi. Meanwhile, the Italian XX Corps was closing in on the port from the south. Several thousand troops of the Indian 4th Division were caught in Benghazi and appeared doomed. But during the night, most of them filtered through German lines to the southeast. They left 1,300 trucks that would serve the Germans well in the months ahead.

Rommel entered the town the following day, January 29, just in time to receive a belated directive from Mussolini, authorizing him to begin the advance on Benghazi. From Hitler came a more timely decree. Evidently unperturbed that Rommel had launched his offensive without informing Berlin, the Führer promoted him to *Generaloberst*, or colonel general.

The remainder of Rommel's January offensive was an anticlimax. Leaving his panzers to refuel and refit, he set out across the Cyrenaic bulge with a pair of moderate-size combat groups composed of truck-borne infantry and armored cars. On February 6, sixteen days after the offensive began, he neared Gazala, more than 250 miles northeast of his starting point and 40 miles short of Tobruk. Aware that the British had regrouped at Gazala and were digging in, Rommel prudently halted his advance to await supplies and reinforcements. "We have got back Cyrenaica," he wrote his wife. "It went like greased lightning."

Fighting had come virtually to a standstill along the new front extending southward from Gazala, and Rommel seized the opportunity to take a month's furlough. His departure for home was a welcome break for the Afrikakorps. "Everybody breathes a huge sigh of relief and looks forward to the coming days of calm," noted the official diary of the 90th Light Division. But Rommel enjoyed little respite. He carried his desert worries everywhere, whether vacationing with his family in Austria or dining with Hitler at the Führer's field headquarters in East Prussia. Rommel assured Hitler that by doubling the Afrikakorps, from three to six divisions, he could conquer Egypt. "Given six German mechanized divisions," Rommel wrote later, "we could have smashed the British so thoroughly that the threat from the south would have been eliminated for a long time to come."

Hitler ruled out that possibility—the extra divisions were needed on the Russian front—so Rommel focused on more immediate objectives. He

A Sudden Thrust to Benghazi

Bolstered by reinforcements reaching his base at El Agheila from Tripoli, Rommel launched a surprise attack on January 21, 1942. Hoping to surround the British 1st Armored Division, he sent his forces northeastward in two columns (*red arrows*). Two days later, the British (*blue arrows*) escaped Rommel's trap east of Agedabia but sustained heavy losses as the panzers pursued them toward Msus. After taking Msus on January 25, Rommel feinted toward Mechili, then led a lightning drive on the port of Benghazi, which fell to his troops on January 29. Over the next week, the panzers swept across Cyrenaica on the heels of the British, who established a new line that ran south from Gazala through Bir Hacheim. On February 6, Rommel stopped to consolidate his gains and prepare for the next confrontation.

asked for sufficient reinforcements to capture the defiant British bastion at Tobruk, which remained a major obstacle along the route to Egypt. And to protect his supply line for the drive on Tobruk, he urged the occupation of Malta, the island stronghold from which British aircraft, ships, and submarines—rejuvenated by flagging German opposition—once more were preying avidly on Axis convoys. Hitler scarcely acknowledged these requests, however, so preoccupied was he with the situation in Russia. Rommel flew back to the desert convinced that, despite his recent triumphs, the Führer still considered North Africa a sideshow.

In fact, Hitler was under increasing pressure to do *something* about Malta. Both Grand Admiral Erich Raeder, the commander of the navy, and Field Marshal Kesselring considered Malta an intolerable drain on their

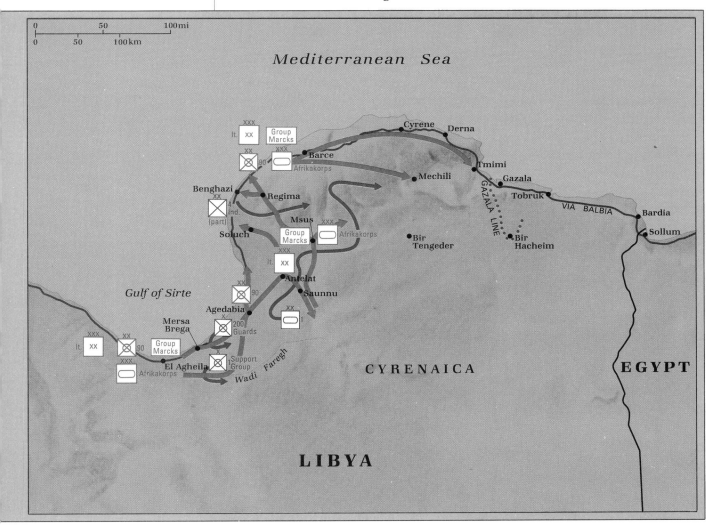

limited resources in the Mediterranean. They urged an immediate invasion. In late February 1942, soon after Rommel's disappointing dinner with the Führer, Kesselring put the case for occupying Malta to Hitler in no uncertain terms. As Kesselring recalled, "Hitler ended the interview by grasping me by the arm and telling me in his Austrian dialect, 'Keep your shirt on, Field Marshal, I'm going to do it!' "

A plan took shape. Dubbed Operation Hercules, it called for an airborne assault even more ambitious than the one directed against the Greek island of Crete in May 1941—a victory whose steep price in German lives still haunted Hitler. Heading up Hercules would be General Kurt Student, commander of the Crete invasion and Germany's preeminent airborne officer, who would commit two paratroop divisions—one German, the other Italian—to quickly seize the island's three airfields and other strategic points. Following that stroke, several seaborne Italian infantry divisions, reinforced with tanks, would hit the beaches to finish off the stranded British garrison.

Above, an exploding German shell narrowly misses a British armored car during Rommel's drive on Benghazi. Below, a panzer pauses at the road junction between Benghazi and Mersa Brega. A hand-lettered sign identifies the place as a watering stop for the British during their recent advance in the opposite direction.

Hercules was scheduled for June. To prepare for it, Kesselring softened up the island with intensified air attacks. Full-scale bombardment began on April 2. Flying from Sicily and the Italian mainland, more than 500 planes of Luftflotte 2 pounded the island. In a month, Kesselring's pilots flew more than 9,500 sorties against Malta and dropped nearly 7,000 tons of bombs. They destroyed docks and repair yards, blew up runways, sank supply ships, and blocked the harbor entrance with mines laid from the air. British surface and submarine flotillas fled the island, and operations at the air bases virtually ceased. By early May, the bombardment was deemed so successful that a large part of Luftflotte 2 returned to the Russian front.

The effect on Rommel's supply line was almost magical. During April, some 150,000 tons of equipment reached his army—more than eight times the amount received the previous month. Axis losses at sea were negligible. Tanks, ammunition, food, gasoline—all poured into Tripoli and the reconditioned ports of Benghazi and Derna on an unprecedented scale. The cargoes even contained an occasional luxury item, such as the portable field toilet with a heart-shaped hole in the door that went to Rommel's staff combat group—the guard for his mobile headquarters. The privy became the envy of every soldier who had to gouge a latrine in the hard desert crust.

The pressure on Malta was beginning to dictate British strategy in North Africa. Prime Minister Winston Churchill wanted his Middle East commander, General Sir Claude Auchinleck, to take the offensive as soon as possible and to recapture the airfields of Cyrenaica so that the RAF, flying from those forward bases, could escort convoys to resupply Malta. Auchinleck held back, stalling for time to enable his field commander at the

front, Lieut. General Neil Ritchie, to work the green units of his Eighth Army into shape and bring up additional tanks and supplies with the help of a railroad extension that now reached from Egypt to Belhamed, twenty miles southeast of Tobruk. Aware of those efforts, Rommel feared that the British would strike before Operation Hercules—the preamble to his Tobruk offensive—was launched in June. A reminder of how quickly the tide of war could turn in the desert greeted him every evening when he returned to his quarters near Derna. The previous occupant, a British soldier, had chalked on the front door: "Please keep tidy. Back soon."

Eager to attack before the British grew too strong, Rommel reversed his order of priorities. Supported by Kesselring, he urged Berlin and Rome to let him move against Tobruk before the invasion of Malta. Hitler and Mussolini, meeting at Berchtesgaden at the end of April, agreed to Rommel's plan. He was to take Tobruk by early June, then halt at the Egyptian border and stay on the defensive while Operation Hercules went forward.

Between Rommel and Tobruk stood a remarkable set of defenses. The British had taken advantage of the respite at the front to establish a line that ran southward from Gazala, on the coast, for forty miles and then angled

In a photograph distributed to much of the world, the Desert Fox reviews his army after it captured Benghazi on January 29, 1942. The presence of Rommel in the forefront, sharing the hardships and hazards of the campaign, cheered his troops, who referred to him familiarly by his first name, Erwin.

back sharply to the northeast for another twenty miles toward Tobruk. The Gazala works featured some of the densest minefields ever sown—half a million mines guarded the approaches to an imposing series of strong-points that the British called boxes.

Spaced at irregular intervals, the boxes were designed to serve as spring-boards for the British summer offensive and as defensive fortresses should Rommel strike first. Each was roughly one mile square, surrounded by barbed wire, and bristling with artillery. Every box held a brigade or more of infantry and enough provisions to withstand a week-long siege. Backing the boxes was Ritchie's mobile reserve: fleets of tanks that could come to the aid of a beleaguered garrison or join it in sallying forth through discrete gaps in the minefields to take the offensive.

The men and weapons guarding the Gazala Line gave the British a significant numerical edge. About 125,000 British troops faced 113,000 Germans and Italians. In addition, the British had about 850 tanks to the enemy's 560, of which 228 were inferior Italian models. To make matters worse for Rommel, the British had ten times as many armored cars as the Axis forces and an advantage of nearly three to two in both artillery and aircraft. German intelligence was aware of some, but not all, of these alarming figures. The full extent of the minefields and the presence or precise positions of at least five British brigades escaped their attention. "Perhaps fortunately, we underestimated the British strength," Mellenthin wrote, "for had we known the full facts, even Rommel might have balked at attacking such a greatly superior enemy."

Rommel could count on a certain edge in quality to help balance the odds against him. On the battlefield, for example, the firepower of his four dozen 88-mm guns and the superiority of his panzers, which were con-centrated to achieve the maximum impact, weighed heavily against the enemy's larger but less cohesive tank force. Overhead, Me 109 fighters could fly rings around the RAF's Hurricanes and Kittyhawks, and the British had nothing to rival the precision bombing of the Stukas. Beyond such tangible assets was the imposing aura that surrounded Rommel himself. For some time, he had been an inspirational figure to his men. "Between Rommel and his troops," noted Mellenthin, "there was a mutual understanding that cannot be explained and analyzed but is a gift of the gods." Now his legend was growing among the British, too. A few months earlier, Churchill had told the House of Commons, "We have a very daring and skillful opponent against us, and, may I say across the havoc of war, a great general."

One of Rommel's secrets was that he did not think or behave like an ordinary general. The British expected Rommel to attack the Gazala Line, with its myriad obstacles, in the conventional manner—head-on. But Rom-

In a photograph taken from an Italian plane, bombs erupt on the terraced fields of Malta, fifteen minutes by air from Sicily.

A Tough Little Island

From roving Phoenician sailors to Napoléon's rapacious legions, generations of intruders had found Malta a morsel as tough as it was tempting. Mixed fortune had strategically placed the rock-bound Mediterranean island group halfway between Gibraltar and Suez and only sixty miles south of Sicily.

After 1815, Great Britain had fortified Malta as a buttress of empire, and by late 1941 planes, ships, and submarines based there had frayed the lifeline linking the Axis nations to their forces in North Africa. Clearly, Malta had to be subdued or the Afrikakorps would be lost.

The modern aggressors were more destructive than any before them. From December 1941 until April 1942, German and Italian bombers swept overhead as many as eight times a day. The resilient Maltese carved air-raid shelters in the islands' abundant limestone, built splinterproof pens to protect their RAF Spitfires—and prayed.

At least some of their prayers were answered: A German bomb, dropped through the dome of a church where 300 parishioners had gathered, miraculously failed to explode. Others did, however, and thousands of buildings—some of them repositories for Malta's renowned art treasures—crumbled under the onslaught.

The vital convoys that sustained Malta were routinely ravaged, and the people soon faced starvation. Fuel, drinking water, and food had to be rationed. "Our diet," wrote the local RAF commander, "was a slice and a half of very poor bread with jam for breakfast, bully beef for lunch with one slice of bread, and the same fare for dinner."

The gritty Maltese, however, once again outlasted their would-be conqueror. The fall of Tobruk and a new German offensive in the Soviet Union distracted Hitler. He shelved plans to invade Malta and shifted the Luftwaffe to other targets.

Smoke billows from an Allied ship bombed in Malta's Grand Harbor, a major base for the British Mediterranean Fleet.

Soldiers clear a bombed-out street in the capital. In April 1942, Axis planes dropped almost 7,000 tons of explosives on Malta.

mel, as he put his troops through last-minute training that included the art of assaulting prepared positions, decided that he would merely feign the expected frontal attack. While infantry units mounted that diversion to preoccupy the British armor, he intended to lead his tank columns and motorized divisions in a daring sweep around the southern flank. Once in the rear of the Gazala Line, he would head for the sea to cut off the British before they could fall back upon Tobruk. He would then isolate the enemy units and destroy them piecemeal. His plan confidently called for attacking Tobruk on the third day of the offensive.

Rommel's decision to send the bulk of his armor around the southern flank abounded with risk. Every bullet and shell, every jerry can of fuel and water, would have to reach Rommel's panzers via that roundabout route. And committing so much of his strength to the flanking move would leave the center of the German line open for a British breakthrough to the west. "If he lost this battle," remarked the Panzerarmee's chief of staff, Lieut. General Alfred Gause, "he stood to lose all Africa."

Rommel launched his offensive—code-named Operation Venezia—in the afternoon on May 26. At two o'clock, a deceptive burst of activity erupted along a twenty-mile front in the northern and central sectors of the Gazala Line. Rommel's artillery thundered. Stukas screamed down on the forward boxes, held by the South African 1st Division and the British 50th Division. Combat engineers crawled forward to probe the treacherous earth and clear lanes through the carpets of mines. Behind them rattled the rifles and machine guns of four Italian infantry divisions and a brigade from the German 90th Light Division, all under the capable command of Lieut. General Ludwig Crüwell, former chief of the Afrikakorps, who had returned to the front after a bout with jaundice. Farther back, Rommel conjured up a spectacular show of armored strength. In fact, only a few tanks were on the scene, but accompanying them was a realistic-looking fleet of mock panzers mounted on automobiles and a new wrinkle in desert-war sleight of hand: airplane engines installed in the rear of trucks to stir up billowing clouds of dust and create the illusion of oncoming columns of armor.

For all its ingenuity, however, the drama was largely lost on the foe it was intended to impress. Thanks to an intercepted German communiqué decoded by Ultra, the British knew an offensive was imminent and were primed to respond. Their edginess could have worked to Rommel's advantage, but the Axis infantry jabs alone offered no proof that the big punch was on the way, and the panzer show was obscured by an afternoon sandstorm, so the British commanders failed to take their cue and move up armor to meet the supposed frontal attack. At the same time, however,

The revving engines of Luftwaffe planes raise a cloud of sand on an airfield seized during the German winter offensive. The two long-range Me 110 fighters parked at near left flew cover for the Ju 52 transports, which delivered a precious cargo of fuel to Rommel's panzers.

the sandstorm provided perfect cover for Rommel's main strike force, which assembled opposite the center of the Gazala Line.

At 10:30 that night, Rommel launched his prodigious armada, numbering roughly 10,000 vehicles in all—tanks and armored cars and trucks bearing sleepy infantrymen and a four-day supply of food, water, and ammunition. His forces advanced southeastward in three columns: The Trieste and Ariete Divisions of the Italian XX Corps were on the left, the 15th and 21st Panzer Divisions in the center, and the 90th Light Division on the right. "I was tense and keyed up, impatiently awaiting the next day," wrote Rommel, who rode along with the panzer divisions. "What would the enemy do? What had he already done?"

Before contending with the enemy, however, Rommel's columns had to cope with the hazards of a nighttime journey across the trackless desert. A single panzer division on the move covered an area of eleven square miles, and moving five divisions through the darkness in concert required intricate orchestration. Moonlight helped, as did the lanterns concealed in gasoline tins that marked the early stages of the intended route. In the distance, German planes dropped flares to delineate the southernmost bastion of the Gazala Line, Bir Hacheim. Duly warned, the ghostly columns gave the box a wide berth. To aid in navigation, the drivers of all vehicles operated on precise compass bearings and maintained a constant speed. Despite the precautions, some units strayed. The Trieste Division, on the far left, wandered to the east of its assigned course and bogged down in sand dunes, leaving its companion unit, Ariete, to go it alone.

Shortly before dawn on May 27, after covering more than thirty miles with few additional mishaps, the army paused for an hour southeast of Bir Hacheim to rest and refuel. Then, having flanked the Gazala Line, the vehicles turned northward. The three columns now diverged to take on their assigned missions *(map, page 113)*. On the left, the Italians made for Bir Hacheim to eliminate that southern anchor of the Gazala Line. On the right, the German 90th Light Division, reinforced by three panzer reconnaissance units, took a northeastward track toward El Adem, fifteen miles south of Tobruk, to deny the British access to their big supply dumps farther east at Belhamed. In the center, the two panzer divisions drove due north. Their ambitious goal was to reach Acroma, a few miles south of the coast highway, that day.

Rommel and his commanders could scarcely believe their good fortune. The British were making no apparent move to counter the massive threat to their rear, and Rommel could only assume that his flanking move had gone undetected. Actually, South African armored cars had been shadowing Rommel's force for some time and reporting by radio to the head-

Lieut. General Ludwig Crüwell *(at center, wearing dark glasses)* briefs German and Italian officers prior to his diversionary attack at Gazala on May 26. Captured by the British three days later, Crüwell was taken to Cairo, where he caught a glimpse of the swank Shepheard's Hotel and quipped to his guards, "It will make a grand headquarters for Rommel."

quarters of the 7th Armored Division. The reports had little impact on a British command structure that was conditioned to expect a frontal assault and inclined to regard anything else as a feint. Soon after daybreak, Rommel's columns began to make contact with exposed enemy units. East of Bir Hacheim, on Rommel's left, elements of the Ariete Division and the 21st Panzer Division surprised the Indian 3d Motor Brigade. Lacking tank support, the brigade swiftly scattered before the onrushing Axis armor.

The panzers then pushed to the north, while the Italians swung west toward their objective, the heavily defended box at Bir Hacheim. Deprived of assistance from the errant Trieste Division, the tank crews of the Ariete Division would have been hard-pressed to break through at Bir Hacheim even with the best of equipment. As it was, they ventured into the mine-fields in flimsy M-13 tanks. Those few M-13s that made it across the fields to the perimeter of the fortress were blasted by antitank guns at point-blank range. The survivors pulled back and regrouped, having lost thirty-two tanks in little more than an hour.

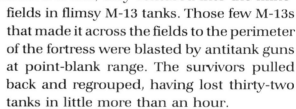

On Rommel's right wing, the 90th Light Division found much easier going. Rumbling along in trucks and armored cars fitted with dust-raising engines in the rear in order to increase their apparent numbers, the Germans paused long enough to compel a small enemy contingent to abandon a box at Retma, then hurried to the north, where they seized the command post of the 7th Armored Division. They even captured the division's commander, Major General Frank Messervy, but did not realize it at the time because he had ripped off his badges of rank; he managed to escape that same night. The ease with which the Germans had neutralized Messervy's isolated division underscored the risk General Ritchie had run by dispersing his armored units—a tactic that Rommel roundly criticized. "The principal aim of the British should have been to bring all the armor they had into action at one and the same time," he asserted after the battle. "They should never have allowed themselves to be duped into dividing their forces."

In truth, both sides had a hard time maintaining cohesion as the battle

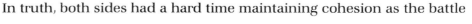

progressed. After seizing Messervy's command post, the 90th Light Division dashed northward, reaching El Adem before noon, but the British were not about to relinquish the route to their supply base without a fight. Ritchie had established a strong box in the area, and before long, British armor was on the way to counter the German threat. In the meantime, the two panzer divisions in the center of Rommel's advance had to make do without their reconnaissance units, which had been detached to strengthen the 90th. Around midmorning, at a point roughly halfway between Bir Hacheim and El Adem, the panzers blundered into a force of about sixty big tanks from the 4th Armored Brigade. The British behemoths scored three quick hits before the Germans brought up a battery of 88-mm flak guns. The 88s blasted the tanks head-on while panzers targeted the enemy flank in a well-coordinated assault that destroyed nearly half of the British armor. The remnants of the enemy brigade fell back toward El Adem, where they exacted some revenge by pounding the 90th Light Division.

After the morning battle, the commander of the 15th Panzer Division, Lieut. General Gustav von Vaerst, hurried to the front of the column as it prepared to resume the advance. A company commander called to him through a megaphone, "Which way now?" Before Vaerst could reply, his adjutant gestured and shouted: "That way! There's Rommel! Follow him!"

Rommel was there indeed, up front as usual, rolling across the debris-littered field in his command vehicle. He could take satisfaction in the familiar tactics of the British, who appeared once again to be committing their armor piecemeal. But he was also disturbed, for among the big tanks that had just challenged his panzers was something new to the desert war: the American-made Grant, a twenty-nine-ton battlewagon assembled in Detroit. At a range of up to 650 yards, the Grant's 75-mm gun could penetrate even the newly thickened front armor of the German mainstay, the Panzer III, and the Grant could deflect shells fired by the Panzer III's short-barreled 50-mm gun from as close as 250 yards. The Grant was more vulnerable to the higher-velocity, long-barreled 50-mm gun on the new Panzer III Special, but Rommel so far had received only nineteen of the Specials. Plainly, his 88-mm batteries would be pressed to the limit in the days ahead. Even after losing sixteen Grants to superior German tactics that morning, the British could still muster 151 of the American machines.

Rommel's worst fears about the new weapon were realized before the day was out. Through the early afternoon, the 15th and 21st Panzer Divisions advanced northward on roughly parallel paths, with the 21st on the left. Around four o'clock, the 15th was nearing the British box known as Knightsbridge, behind the center of the Gazala Line, when forty Grant tanks, supported by heavily armored Matildas, slammed into the division's

A Perilous End Run at Gazala

JUNE 5–JUNE 6

MINEFIELDS

SIDRA RIDGE

KNIGHTSBRIDGE BOX

THE CAULDRON

ASLAGH RIDGE

Ariete

Bir el Harmat

MAY 26–MAY 28, 1942

Sabratha

Trento

Brescia

Pavia

Afrika-korps

Trieste
(in error)

Ariete

Gazala

VIA BALBIA

COMMONWEALTH KEEP
(HILL 209)

Acroma

AXIS BYPASS

Tobruk

KING'S CROSS

1 SA

50

32

THE CAULDRON

GOT EL UALEB

150

Bir el Harmat

22

201 Guards

KNIGHTSBRIDGE

2

El Adem

Belhamed

Sidi Rezegh

9 Ind. (part)

Fr.

Bir Hacheim

3 Ind.

21

15

Retma

7

7 Armd.

4

29 Ind.

Bir el Gubi

0   10   20mi
0   10   20km

Late on May 26, following a feint
by Crüwell's infantry, Rommel
led his mobile units around the
British army's southern flank at
Gazala to drive a wedge between
it and his goal, Tobruk. On
May 27, heavy fighting erupted.
The Italian Ariete Division failed
to take the Free French bastion
at Bir Hacheim; the 90th Light

tore through the British 7th
Armored Division's headquarters
before halting near El Adem; the
15th and 21st Panzer encountered enemy tanks and stopped
short of Acroma. Over the next
two days, Rommel struggled to
maintain his supply conduit.
Then on May 30 he tried to break
through the British line in an

area known afterward as the
Cauldron. Blocked by a fortified
garrison, he stormed the
redoubt, capturing it on June 1.
Four days later, the British
launched an abortive effort to
crush the panzers in the
Cauldron (inset). Rommel then
besieged Bir Hacheim until the
defenders withdrew on June 10.

rear. The German columns staggered under the impact. Panzers took hit after hit while their own missiles bounced harmlessly off the Grants' thick frontal plates. The surprise attack exposed the division's truck drivers to worse fire than they had ever seen. Many of them panicked and drove wildly to the south and west. Motorized infantry units took terrible losses in the melee, and divisional and regimental staffs were thrown into chaos. Even Rommel's elite staff combat group was caught up in the confusion. "It's a massacre," one of Rommel's aides wrote in his diary. "Our squad reels first to the left and then to the right. It's terrible."

The acting Afrikakorps commander, Lieut. General Walther Nehring, found himself in the middle of the stampede with the head of the 135th Flak Regiment, Colonel Alwin Wolz, at his side. He ordered Wolz to bring up his 88-mm guns to counter the British tanks. Wolz looked around the swirling frenzy of trucks and guns and spotted some idle 88s. "We raced over to them," he said later, "and suddenly found Rommel there, completely hemmed in by panicking troops. He angrily rebuked me that my flak was to blame for all this, because it was not shooting back." Stung, Wolz moved several of the big guns into line in time to confront the enemy. "The armada of enemy tanks was closing in and only 1,500 yards away," Wolz recalled. He counted forty big tanks, all driving defenseless supply trucks before them. "In the midst of this chaos were Rommel, the headquarters of the Afrikakorps, regimental staffs, signals trucks—in short, the entire nerve center of the combat divisions was up front."

With no time to spare, Wolz's hastily assembled 88s lashed out at the oncoming armor. The Grant made a good target; the tall vehicle had to expose its hull when firing because its main gun was mounted there rather than in the turret, which was taken up by a smaller 37-mm gun. Before long, several of the big tanks had been hit and were belching smoke. But the British re-formed and came on again. Meanwhile, Wolz had restored order to his flak regiment and was extending his line. Soon he had a screen of sixteen 88s deployed over a front two miles wide. Braving their fire, a few of the British tanks made it to the muzzles of the 88s and blew away the crews. As British artillery joined in, Wolz's line was in danger of crumbling. But then—with typical Rommel luck—a sandstorm blew up, obscuring the 88s and the panzers they were protecting. The flak front held, and the British pulled back, leaving twenty-four shattered tanks on the field.

Following the fierce battle, the Germans could do little but push a few miles farther north and stop for the night. Some of those who had narrowly escaped death that afternoon—including men of the hard-hit motorized infantry units—took the opportunity to celebrate their reprieve. May 27 happened to be the birthday of a lieutenant named Paulewiecz, a company

A British crew surrenders after emerging from a crippled Grant tank—a powerful American-built weapon that made its debut at Gazala on May 27. With a 75-mm cannon that was mounted on its hull, the Grant could outgun most German tanks, but it fared little better than its British counterparts against Rommel's potent 88-mm artillery.

commander in the 104th Regiment. His men had captured a British truck laden with beer and whiskey, and they drank to his health and long life. Another lieutenant of the motorized infantry, Heinz Schmidt, was the sole surviving officer of the 115th Regiment's devastated 2d Battalion. During a lull just before the battle, Schmidt had shot a wild gazelle and had been roasting it over a fire of gasoline and cleaning rags down in a small wadi when the British tanks overran his position. Schmidt took shelter in a ditch and escaped detection, but of the 350 men in his unit, only 30 eluded death, wounding, or capture. After the battle, Schmidt crawled from his hiding place and returned to the well-roasted venison. "I can still remember the feeling of the juice running down from the corners of my mouth," he wrote later. "It was good to be alive."

Rommel took no comfort from such simple pleasures that Wednesday night. At his mobile headquarters, near the front line of his embattled panzer divisions, he pondered the situation: His daring plan to flank the Gazala Line and quickly destroy it from behind had foundered. Instead of

scattering the British, his own army was scattered, and the pieces were in danger of encirclement. Near El Adem, the 4th Armored Brigade had kept the 90th Light Division pinned down since early afternoon; it was out of radio contact and threatened from the air. The Ariete Division was licking its wounds near Bir Hacheim, while Free French patrols from that strongpoint roamed the southern flank and disrupted Rommel's supply line. Farther north, Rommel's panzers had halted about eight miles short of Acroma, their objective for the day. More than a third of their tanks had been knocked out, and the 15th Division was practically out of gas because its supply columns lagged far behind. "I will not deny," Rommel conceded afterward, "that I was seriously worried."

The second morning of the battle began inauspiciously for the anxious commander of Panzerarmee Afrika. "Shortly after dawn, British tanks opened fire on my command post," Rommel reported. "Shells fell all around us, and the wind-screen of our command vehicle flew into fragments." Rommel and his staff managed to retreat safely out of enemy range, but the incident set the tone for the day. On his right, the 90th Light Division fell back under persistent pressure from enemy tanks and planes. To his left and rear, the situation remained precarious. The Italian units were unable to mount a sustained attack, and his supply columns were subject to repeated raids. In the center, only the 21st Panzer Division—led by Major General Georg von Bismarck in an aggressive manner befitting his name—made any headway. The 15th Panzer Division spent the day waiting in vain for fuel. By evening, the division's inactivity so concerned Rommel that he made a dangerous trek to the southwest to patch up his frayed supply line. At dawn the next day, May 29, he led forward to the stalled panzers a convoy of trucks loaded with gas.

In this instance, Rommel's penchant for leading from the front paid major dividends. But such direct intervention at Gazala created enormous command problems. During his frequent forays, Rommel sometimes lost contact even with his own mobile headquarters and was thus out of touch both with his scattered ground forces and with the Luftwaffe, which depended on his instructions to allocate its resources. Kesselring, who was on hand to coordinate the Luftwaffe's activities with Rommel, noted that the confusion at headquarters on May 28 "beggared all description."

Kesselring's patience with Rommel was further tested the next day, when he stepped in as a temporary replacement for General Ludwig Crüwell, the commander of the Italian and German infantry west of the Gazala Line, who had been shot down on a reconnaissance flight that morning and taken prisoner. The emergency thrust Kesselring into a pe-

culiar position. A fifty-six-year-old field marshal whose own knack for getting close to the action led him to fly nearly 200 reconnaissance missions over the Gazala Line, he subordinated himself to Rommel, who was his junior in rank and age, but chafed at finding his hands tied by subservience to "a headquarters that issues no orders and cannot be reached."

If Rommel's immersion in the flow of the battle sometimes maddened his senior officers, it often inspired his troops, and it enabled him to sense the shifting current of events at the front and respond accordingly. While his British opponents endlessly debated at headquarters in the rear about where and how to crush the Axis advance, Rommel was on the spot and improvising. Late on May 29, when his various forces were still intact but desperate for supplies, Rommel offered fresh proof of his flexibility by radically altering his plans. Having led his divisions in a vast arc around the Gazala Line, he decided that the only way to prevent their destruction and divide the enemy was to complete the circle. Temporarily forsaking his drive against Tobruk, he would concentrate his dispersed forces behind the middle of the Gazala Line and break through the intervening minefields from east to west, thus restoring his supply conduit and severing the British line in one deft stroke.

The target for this thrust was an area in the Gazala Line about fifteen miles north of Bir Hacheim. Around a saucerlike depression the Arabs called Got el Ualeb, there appeared to be a broad gap in the British box system. On the far side of this zone, troops of the Trieste Division, which had gone astray on the first night of the offensive, had begun the tortuous process of clearing a lane eastward through the minefields in the area. To link up with them, Rommel had squads probe westward on the morning of May 30 while he established a shield of 88s and panzers to protect against the enemy armor pressing from the north and east. That afternoon, two British tank brigades tried to break through this screen but were driven off. Meanwhile, the Germans and Italians made contact in the minefields. Their risky work yielded two parallel corridors, approximately six miles apart, on either side of the depression.

Rommel's troops then made a shocking discovery. Nestled in the saucer of Got el Ualeb, between the cleared lanes, was a British box that German reconnaissance had somehow failed to detect. Several thousand British troops of the 150th Brigade, supported by eighty Matildas, held the strongpoint. Artillery in the box commanded both Axis corridors and made it practically impossible to move convoys through them. Irrevocably committed to his new plan, Rommel resolved to destroy the box. The ensuing battles, contested amid the choking dust and searing heat, were so intense the area became known as the Cauldron.

After surrounding the British bastion, Rommel attacked early on May 31 with elements of three divisions. The Axis forces "fought their way forward yard by yard," Rommel wrote, "against the toughest British resistance imaginable." The day ended with no sign of surrender from the besieged garrison. Rommel's supply situation was now so critical that his aides were thinking the unthinkable. "We were in a really desperate position, our backs against the minefield, no food, no water, no petrol, very little ammunition," recalled Colonel Fritz Bayerlein, chief of staff of the Afrikakorps. When a captured British officer complained to Rommel that evening that the prisoners were not getting enough water, Rommel asserted that they were getting "the same ration of water as the Afrikakorps and myself—half a cup." As the officer recalled, Rommel went on to imply that he would have to capitulate—"ask for terms" is the way he put it—if no convoy made it through by noon the next day.

The following morning, June 1, Rommel threw everything he could muster at the gallant men inside the box. His artillery flung in round after round; Stukas screamed down from the sky; panzers rumbled in close. Sappers from the 104th Infantry Regiment led their comrades through the last belt of mines, and men from the regiment's 3d Battalion advanced into the British positions. The battle was still raging when Rommel approached the contested area about noon—his self-imposed deadline—to confer with the battalion's acting commander, Captain Werner Reissmann.

"I think they've had enough, Reissmann!" he shouted. "Wave to them with white flags—they'll surrender!" Reissmann was skeptical, but Rommel waved a white flag, and the opposing troops answered with handkerchiefs and scarves. One Tommy took off his shirt and wagged it wildly. The firing ebbed, and the exhausted defenders crawled out of their foxholes and trenches with hands in the air. Nearly 3,000 British troops surrendered that day. Rommel's lifelines through the Gazala minefields were now secure.

The response of the British field commander, General Ritchie, was baffling. During the battle in the Cauldron, he had declined the opportunity to assault the vulnerable Axis army there. Convinced that Rommel was retreating, Ritchie was busy developing a grandiose scheme to pursue him on the far side of the Gazala Line. As late as June 2, the day after the surrender, he signaled Auchinleck in Cairo that the situation was "favorable to us and getting better daily."

Not until June 5 did Ritchie mount a major effort to dislodge Rommel from the Cauldron. It was doomed from its start, before dawn, when a massive artillery barrage fell harmlessly on the empty desert—the result of faulty reconnaissance. Two Indian infantry brigades and an armored brigade then attacked from the east while another tank brigade approached

Cutting across recent tracks in the sand, Free French troops venture from Bir Hacheim in a Bren gun carrier to harry German convoys. Such sorties confirmed the comment by a Rommel aide that the Axis May 27 assault on Bir Hacheim had been "far too casual."

from the north in an ill-coordinated assault that brought to bear only about half the available forces. "If ever an operation resembled sticking one's arm into a wasp's nest," a British commander remarked, "this did." Swarming from the Cauldron, the panzers beat back the assault to the north and then overwhelmed the forces to the east. As Rommel reported with satisfaction, "Soon the guns of our tanks were firing from three sides into the British, who fought back in their usual way, with extreme stubbornness but far too little mobility." On this day and the next, the British lost more than 200 tanks and 4,000 prisoners of war around the seething Cauldron.

Among the captives was a brigadier named Desmond Young. When British shellfire began falling on the column of POWs and their guards, a German officer ordered Young to go with an escort under a flag of truce to tell the battery to stop firing. Young refused, and as the two men stood there arguing, Rommel drove up and ruled in favor of the prisoner. Young was so impressed that he offered Rommel one acknowledgment on the spot—a smart salute—and another eight years later, when he wrote the first major biography of this legendary enemy.

After the Cauldron was well in hand, Rommel moved south to deal with Bir Hacheim. On June 2, that nettlesome strongpoint at the southern tip of the crumbling Gazala Line had withstood a second major assault, this one by the infantry of the 90th Light and Trieste Divisions. That the box had not yet collapsed was a tribute both to its unrivaled fortifications and to its unusual defenders. Surrounded by some of the thickest minefields in the entire British network, it contained an estimated 1,200 emplacements for machine guns and antitank guns. And many of its 3,600 troops had a special motivation to resist the enemy. Fighting under the cross of Lorraine, they included partisans of General Charles de Gaulle who had seen their homeland overrun in 1940. Their ranks also numbered Jews and other victims of Nazi persecution who had fled Germany and the occupied countries. Lieutenant Alfred Berndt, the Nazi propagandist on Rommel's staff, sneeringly described them as "Gaullists, swashbucklers, and criminals of twenty different nations."

Their tenacity amazed Rommel. A former infantry commander, he was proud of his skill in leading troops against fortified positions, and he assumed command of the campaign to crack Bir Hacheim. Calculating that tanks would be ineffectual in the minefields there, he left most of his panzers in the Cauldron and brought additional infantry units south to support the 90th Light Division, which renewed its attack on June 6. To blast a path for the foot soldiers, Rommel's gunners poured in torrents of shells while the Luftwaffe flew hundreds of sorties against Bir Hacheim in the face of furious resistance by the RAF. Three days passed with scarcely

Hammering Through to Tobruk

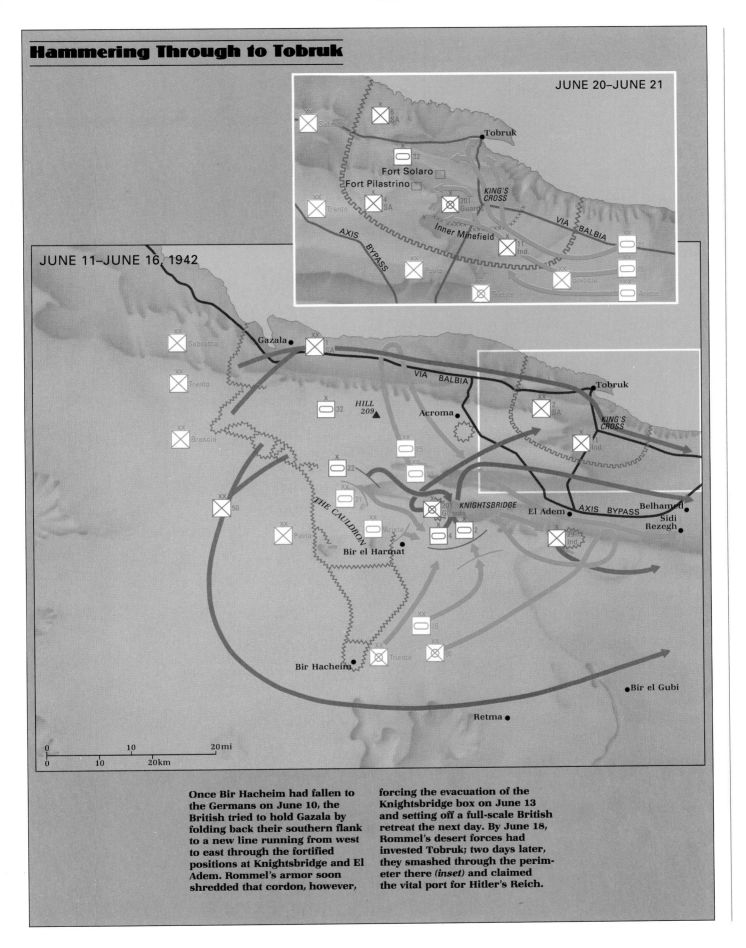

JUNE 20–JUNE 21

JUNE 11–JUNE 16, 1942

Once Bir Hacheim had fallen to the Germans on June 10, the British tried to hold Gazala by folding back their southern flank to a new line running from west to east through the fortified positions at Knightsbridge and El Adem. Rommel's armor soon shredded that cordon, however, forcing the evacuation of the Knightsbridge box on June 13 and setting off a full-scale British retreat the next day. By June 18, Rommel's desert forces had invested Tobruk; two days later, they smashed through the perimeter there *(inset)* and claimed the vital port for Hitler's Reich.

a break in the storm, and still the defenders refused to give up. "In the whole course of the desert war," wrote Mellenthin, newly promoted to operations chief for Rommel's army, "we never encountered a more heroic and better-sustained defense."

For Field Marshal Kesselring, who had resumed his overall responsibility for the Luftwaffe at Gazala, the prospect of a prolonged siege at Bir Hacheim was appalling. In one twenty-four-hour period there, he had seen nearly forty of his Stukas shot down by the RAF—losses that, if sustained for any length of time, would leave him too weak to support the coming drive on Tobruk or the subsequent attack on Malta. On June 9, he implored Rommel to commit his panzers in an all-out assault on the bastion—a proposal Rommel rejected as an invitation to disaster.

Finally, on June 10, the relentless German pressure on Bir Hacheim began to tell. "Another hellish day," one of the defenders scrawled in his diary. "A bombing raid at nine, another at ten, and the rattle of machine-gun fire all day long. The stink of corpses is just unbearable and saps all our powers of resistance." That night, exhausted from their two-week ordeal, out of water and ammunition, and threatened by an assault group that had penetrated their northern perimeter, the defenders gave up the struggle in a manner consistent with their defiant stand. Detecting a gap in the German lines to the west, some 2,700 of them slipped through in the dark and achieved a rendezvous with trucks and ambulances from the 7th Motor Brigade. The other 500 survivors, most of them too badly wounded to escape, surrendered the next morning. To Rommel's credit, he treated all of them as prisoners of war, ignoring a secret order from Hitler that the Germans among them were to be "terminated with extreme prejudice."

Having unhinged the Gazala Line, Rommel could at last revert to his original objective. In his order for the day on June 11, he put it tersely: "Tobruk. Everything for Tobruk." To eliminate the remaining obstacles that separated him from the port, he dispatched the forces that had besieged Bir Hacheim in a fan-shaped movement toward the British boxes at Knightsbridge and El Adem while the 21st Panzer and Ariete Divisions moved eastward from the Cauldron. In response, Ritchie pulled back his left flank so that the truncated Gazala defenses now formed an L. The old line extended about twenty miles south from the sea, and the new leg jutted eastward through Knightsbridge and El Adem.

Both sides were exhausted after two weeks of battle. Rommel bemoaned his shortage of foot soldiers, a condition exacerbated by his steep losses at Bir Hacheim. The 90th Light Division emerged from that struggle with no more than a thousand men fit for duty—roughly the strength of a

After the fall of Bir Hacheim, a trench covered with camouflage netting remains intact amid the scattered munitions crates and other debris. A British defender of Bir Hacheim wrote that many "trenches and walls of the fort caved in, burying men alive."

regiment. The British, despite their setbacks, still had more tanks than the Germans, thanks to reinforcements from Cairo. But that edge was dulled not only by the lack of compatibility within their armored units—which contained as many as five different types of tank—but by the continued lack of coordination among units. Over the next two days, Rommel's panzer divisions repeatedly outmaneuvered the British tank brigades in a series of fiery encounters that obliterated Ritchie's flimsy hopes.

The crucial battle occurred around the Knightsbridge box, where the British 2d and 4th Armored Brigades—under Messervy, the general who had been taken prisoner on May 27 only to escape that night—stood in the way of the 15th Panzer Division, advancing from the south. On the morning of June 12, Messervy left his position to confer briefly with his corps commander at headquarters. Along the way, however, Messervy ran afoul of his former nemesis: A probing column of the 90th Light Division spotted

German infantrymen sprawl on
the sand after penetrating the
perimeter of Tobruk on June 20,
1942, on the heels of a furious
bombardment delivered at dawn
that day by Stukas and artillery.

his car, and he had to abandon the vehicle and take shelter in an empty water cistern to avoid being captured a second time. It took a few hours for his disappearance to register at headquarters, and by the time another officer was dispatched to take charge of Messervy's brigades, they were under attack. The 15th Panzer Division was advancing head-on from the south, the 21st weighing in unexpectedly from the west. Outflanked and bereft of their commander, the battered brigades fell back to a position east of Knightsbridge, exposing that box. The next day, June 13, the panzers continued their relentless envelopment of the position, leaving the garrison there—which had held out stubbornly for more than two weeks—with little choice but to withdraw from the box that night, while they still had a chance to escape. When Knightsbridge was abandoned, Ritchie's new line crumbled. The vain effort to hold it had cost him nearly 140 tanks, leaving him with just 70, or less than half Rommel's number.

On June 14, as his southern front fell to tatters, Ritchie finally ordered evacuation of the two divisions that had defended the northern part of the line from the beginning. His order set in motion a dash for safety that would be remembered as the "Gazala Gallop." One division, the British 50th, found itself too far south to attempt to reach the best route eastward, the Via Balbia, near the coast. Its commander, Major General W. H. Ramsden, chose the same way out that Rommel had taken in. That night, his men fought a few miles westward through the Italian infantry fronting them and then

A German battery *(right)* joins the barrage that detonated mines protecting Tobruk in a chain reaction, blasting a path that enabled German troops to break through to the Mediterranean.

hurried southward around Bir Hacheim. The flight toward the Egyptian frontier went so smoothly, Ramsden reported, that "we stopped in the desert for a brew-up."

Near the coast, meanwhile, there was no time for tea as the South African 1st Division sped eastward on the Via Balbia late on June 14. The Luftwaffe, which might have blocked the escape, had been called away to bomb a British convoy bound for Malta. Rommel lashed his panzers northward all day in a race to cut the highway and trap the South Africans. To reach the coast highway, the panzers had to blast through the remnants of the British armor. The struggle so drained the Germans that they stopped short of the highway at nightfall and slept, despite Rommel's urgent orders to continue. Most of the South Africans made it through to safety before dawn.

After a night's rest, the revived tank crews took up the pursuit at full throttle, severing the highway and pushing to the Mediterranean before veering eastward. Late on June 16, Rommel's men claimed the remaining

In captured Tobruk, Germans smile from their car outside a barber shop frequented until that day by the British. With dark humor, the British had named the shop for Sweeney Todd, the London barber of legend who slit his clients' throats.

strongpoint on Ritchie's decimated line—El Adem, south of Tobruk. The next day, the last British armored units followed the retreating infantry across the frontier into Egypt after losing thirty-two more tanks to enemy fire or mechanical breakdown. On June 18, Rommel completed the investment of Tobruk on its three landward sides. "To each one of us, Tobruk was a symbol of British resistance," he said, "and we were now going to finish with it for good."

Only in superficial ways did Tobruk resemble the fortress that Rommel had failed to crack in eight months of trying the year before. It was still girded by a thirty-mile-long protective perimeter and defended by a garrison of nearly 35,000 troops. But the antitank ditch had been allowed to silt up, and many of the mines had been transplanted to the Gazala Line. In contrast to the battle-hardened Australians who had withstood Rommel's siege the previous spring, the garrison now consisted mainly of untried troops of the South African 2d Division, along with two infantry brigades and an armored brigade that were worn out from the Gazala battles. The defenders were short on tanks and antitank guns. In fact, British commanders had long ago decided not to attempt to withstand another siege—a decision that went by the boards when Churchill handed down a last-minute injunction to hold Tobruk "at all costs."

Confident of success, Rommel dusted off the plan he had developed the previous November, before Auchinleck's offensive had preempted a renewed assault on Tobruk. Indulging his flair for deception, Rommel drove his mobile forces toward the frontier as if pursuing the enemy into Egypt. Then, while the 90th Light Division kept up the feint by pressing on to the coastal town of Bardia, he suddenly wheeled his panzers about and drove hellbent for Tobruk. As his forces moved into position southeast of the fortress that night, they found undisturbed old supply dumps containing artillery shells that they had cached there the last time around. And as they shivered in the chill desert air before the dawn attack, many veterans had to endure negative memories as well—dark, nagging thoughts of their previous failures at Tobruk.

A devastatingly effective artillery and air bombardment began the assault precisely at 5:20 a.m. on June 20. Kesselring, eager to take Tobruk and then invade the island of Malta, mustered more than 150 bombers from North Africa, Sicily, Greece, and Crete. Wave after wave dropped nearly 400 tons of bombs on the southeastern sector of the perimeter, touching off a chain reaction of explosions in the minefields. Infantry surged forward an hour or so after the bombardment began. At 8:30 a.m., the first of Rommel's phalanx of 125 tanks from the 15th and 21st Panzer Divisions rumbled across the silted-up perimeter ditch.

By nine o'clock, the panzers had penetrated so far into the maze of concrete bunkers that Rommel uncharacteristically claimed victory even though the fighting had scarcely begun. He summoned a war correspondent and, while the thump and clatter of battle sounded around him, recorded an announcement for German radio. "Today," he intoned, "my troops have crowned their efforts by capturing Tobruk." Fortunately for Rommel, his forces made good on the boast. By early afternoon, the panzers had covered more than four miles to the key road junction of King's Cross, roughly midway between the perimeter and the harbor. By nightfall, they effectively controlled Tobruk.

The next morning, Rommel rode through the rubble of ruined buildings and the acrid fumes of torched supply dumps to accept the surrender of the South African commandant, Major General H. B. Klopper. Some 33,000 troops flowed into the prisoner-of-war pens. Once again, as he had at Bir Hacheim, Rommel insisted upon treating the captives equally, rejecting a plea from some white South African officers that their black countrymen, who served as ancillary troops, be held in separate quarters.

The conquerors of Tobruk marveled at the booty that fell to them. The bastion had collapsed so quickly that the defenders had time to destroy only a small portion of their supplies, leaving huge amounts of fuel and 2,000 motor vehicles of all kinds—no small compensation for an Axis army that had lost hundreds of tanks and countless other conveyances in the past month. Along with the hardware came priceless incidental goods: tobacco, white flour, tinned food, German beer purchased in neutral Portugal, fresh khaki uniforms—and the desert boots that Rommel's men so coveted. "Shoes, gorgeous shoes," recalled one Italian engineer, "just like those that we had occasionally seen on prisoners—soft, elegant suede shoes with thick rubber soles."

Even the ascetic Rommel was impressed by the epicurean delights that suddenly appeared on his table in Tobruk; he still talked about them two years later. But something far more memorable to Rommel accompanied the capture of this desert port. The day after its surrender, the exhausted commander, who had been living in his command vehicle for nearly a month, went to bed early—only to be awakened by excited members of his staff. They had just heard the news on the evening broadcast from Berlin: A grateful Führer had promoted Rommel to field marshal—at the age of fifty, the youngest German ever to reach that exalted rank. Word of the honor "came like a dream," he wrote Lucie. After savoring the moment with his aides, Rommel returned to bed. His gamble at Gazala had earned him laurels that most generals would have been content to rest on. But the Desert Fox was up at six the next morning, his sights set on Egypt. ✠

A Miserable Place to Fight a War

By day, the desert was so hot that touching the sun-baked metal of a vehicle could result in a serious burn. At night, the temperature dropped so precipitately that, "even with three blankets," a soldier described, "one is frozen like a naked ski instructor." The climate's contrasts were only part of the misery the desert inflicted on the Afrikakorps. It was as though nature had conspired with the usual snafus of army supply to make the lives of Rommel's men thoroughly wretched.

Among the most persistent natural enemies was the fine sand. "We have more sand than hair on our heads," one German wrote home. The gritty stuff plugged nostrils and got into wounds, preventing them from healing. When whipped by southern winds, the grains swirled into a sandstorm—called a ghibli by the Arabs—so maddening that Bedouin law excused a husband for killing his wife after he endured five days of it. The sand caused weapons to jam and engines to seize up, paralyzing the supply lines on which the troops depended for food, water, and clothing. "The last time I saw my feet was in Brindisi," recorded a diarist, exercising a soldier's prerogative to exaggerate after more than a year in the field. "There are no more changes of socks, so what's the point of taking off a useless pair when I must put them on again?"

Vermin added to the woe. A bite from the horned viper—named for the protuberances on its head—had to be tied off and cut open to drain the poison. Similar treatment was necessary for the sting of the yellow scorpion, which often nested in soldiers' boots. Leeches lurked in the water dipped from cisterns. And the ticklike sand flea, so tiny it was barely visible when it leaped onto a person, dug into the skin and sucked blood until it swelled into a round, thick ball. "Many men had to be sent home," noted a German official, "because the sand fleas drove them half out of their minds."

The biggest problem was water—or the lack of it. It reached most troops only by truck and was strictly rationed—usually three quarts per man per day. Even Rommel complained of the scarcity. "One's thirst," he conceded, "becomes almost unquenchable."

A veteran Afrikakorps member is wrapped like a mummy beneath tight-fitting goggles in order to protect his face and eyes from the stinging desert sand.

A Minimum of Food and Shelter

The inexperience that plagued Germany's desert warriors was epitomized by field ovens such as the one at left: They burned wood, which had to be shipped to the treeless battle zone all the way from Italy. Much of the food came from Italy, too. Because white bread and potatoes would spoil in shipment, the troops instead received dry legumes and zwieback and brown bread wrapped in wax paper. Occasionally, the men relieved the tedium of their diet by shooting a desert gazelle (*above, left*) or other wild game. And a regular ration of vitamin pills helped to make up for the lack of fresh fruits and vegetables. Tented slit trenches (*above*) provided some warmth at night but became so hot in the daytime, wrote one man, that they were "only really useful for hatching eggs."

Precious water, shipped from coastal desalination plants or sucked from desert wells, was stored at distribution depots (above). Then it was trucked to the front in metal containers that came to be known as jerry cans (right), from the British slang for Germans. Cans marked with a white cross were to be filled with water only, but because of mix-ups the water often tasted of gasoline. It was welcomed anyway. Usually, soldiers had no water to spare for laundry and used sand to scour their clothes (left). But Lieutenant Ralf Ringler recalled receiving his first can of water in ten days. "First of all, a hearty slug, then I washed my face—divine!" After Ringler had shaved and bathed, a little more than a quart remained as a murky soup. "Throw it away? Not on your life! First a handkerchief, then my shirt, and finally in the thick dark soup I soaked the tatters of my socks. What a day! I came out of it like a man reborn."

Enduring a Desert Hurricane

A swirling ghibli engulfs a German patrol, blotting out the sun and halting all fighting save the battle to survive the hurricane-

force winds and the lacerating power of the driving sand.

FOUR

Days of Decision at El Alamein

ow for the complete destruction of the enemy," declared the Wehrmacht's newest field marshal in an exultant order of the day on June 21, 1942. Erwin Rommel went on to congratulate his men for their victory at Tobruk and vowed that his desert panzers would not rest "until we have shattered the last remnants of the British Eighth Army. During the days to come, I shall call on you for one more great effort to bring us to this final goal."

Before this effort could begin, however, Rommel had to fight a preliminary skirmish with his superiors to have his orders changed. The original plan, drawn up in late April, called for Panzerarmee Afrika to halt before crossing the frontier into Egypt so that the Luftwaffe could be diverted from the desert campaign to support an airborne invasion of Malta. A succession of German air raids during April had all but subdued the island, but once the raids stopped, the RAF and Royal Navy units based there had quickly revived. RAF squadrons operating from Maltese bases were again sinking ships carrying supplies to Rommel's army, and Axis troops were once more feeling the resultant shortages in gasoline and ammunition. Field Marshal Albert Kesselring, backed by Rommel's nominal superior, Marshal Ettore Bastico, urged Rommel to halt his pursuit of the Eighth Army and allow Malta to be captured as planned.

Rommel, eager to seize what he saw as a glittering opportunity, would have none of it. He insisted that the attack on Malta be postponed so the Luftwaffe could support his thrust to Suez; any delay, he argued, would give the British time to shore up their strength. Kesselring was equally adamant, and he was backed by the Italian command and German naval chiefs. The argument became heated when both commanders refused to yield. Rommel played his trump card, dispatching an aide to Berlin to plead his case with Hitler—successfully, as it turned out. (Kesselring complained afterward about Rommel's "almost hypnotic influence" over Hitler.) The Führer signaled his decision to Mussolini, adding that "it is only once in a lifetime that the goddess of victory smiles."

Tanks and trucks in the vanguard of the Axis offensive rumbled across

German infantrymen trudge toward El Alamein, where the British had dug in to stop them in July 1942. Hemmed in and short of gasoline, Rommel's desert troops resigned themselves, in the words of one officer, "to the dreariness and deadliness of static warfare."

the border into Egypt on the evening of June 23. "We're on the move and hope to land the next big punch very soon," Rommel wrote to his wife that night. "Speed is the main thing now." Two days later, the army's advance units reached the defenses of the coastal town Mersa Matruh. The Germans moved so quickly that they soon outran their supply elements. Tanks of the 21st Panzer Division stranded their own supply trucks by siphoning off fuel to keep moving. The panzers finally had to halt, harried relentlessly by the British Desert Air Force. General Sir Claude Auchinleck, who now took over direct command of the Eighth Army, had deployed his British and Commonwealth troops on a line extending from Mersa Matruh, on the Mediterranean, to an escarpment called Sidi Hamza, twenty miles to the southwest. Thousands of mines were planted in front of the British positions.

Although his army was outnumbered in both men and tanks, Rommel counted on the tactics that had always served him well—speed, mobility, and surprise. Unfortunately, this very speed meant that the understrength Luftwaffe could not establish forward bases in the desert quickly enough to provide effective air cover. Even so—and with only the scantiest information about British troop dispositions in hand—Rommel attacked on the afternoon of June 26. His 21st Panzer and 90th Light Divisions, striking at the center of the British line, were surprised to discover that they had hit the defenders' weak point.

As it happened, Auchinleck expected Rommel to strike his flanks in an effort to encircle and cut off the Allied forces. Consequently, the British

A death's-head (*above*) marks a tank trap of concrete barriers and buried mines guarding the British bastion at Mersa Matruh. Avoiding such snares, Rommel's forces outflanked the line and pulled down the Union Jack at Mersa Matruh (*right*) on June 29.

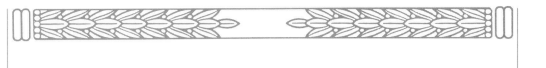

general deployed most of his strength at the two ends of his line. To the north, he placed the Indian X Corps, consisting of the British 50th and Indian 10th Divisions. To the south, at the escarpment, he stationed the two divisions of the XIII Corps: his mobile 1st Armored, with the New Zealand 2d behind it. Two brigades of the 7th Armored Division stiffened the position. The ten or so miles between these two strong anchors were lightly mined and defended by scattered strongpoints of mixed infantry and artillery.

The attacking German divisions routed the thin detachments in their path and sliced deep into British territory, the 90th Light veering north toward the coast road, the 21st Panzer pushing southeastward. Rommel himself led the 21st Panzer the next day as its tanks worked around the New Zealand 2d and 1st Armored from the north and attacked from the rear. At the same time, the 15th Panzer Division, on Rommel's southern flank, smashed into the 1st Armored's front. Rommel's audacity was paying off yet again; the 21st Panzer possessed only 23 tanks and 600 men and yet was bringing to bay a vastly more powerful enemy—the reinforced 1st Armored Division alone had 159 tanks. Had those tanks attacked in support of the New Zealanders, the 21st Panzer might have been annihilated. Although they had halted the advance of the 15th Panzer, the British commanders grew edgy in the face of the Germans' lightning stab. Concerned that his XIII Corps might be cut off, General W. H. E. Gott ordered a withdrawal.

The New Zealand troops broke through the 21st Panzer Division's lines amid fierce hand-to-hand fighting and joined the 1st Armored in the retreat eastward. The 21st Panzer turned northeast and pushed toward Fuka, a village forty miles southeast of Mersa Matruh. It cut the coast road and captured the heights southwest of the village.

Meanwhile, to the north, the German 90th Light Division had reached the coast road near Gerawla, east of Mersa Matruh, severing the line of retreat of the X Corps, on the British right wing. The men of the 90th prepared to storm the town and its defenses, where much of the corps was now cut off, but the British broke out during the night of June 28 in a wild melee that at one point surged through Rommel's mobile headquarters. High-ranking German staff officers grabbed submachine guns as British infantrymen raced pell-mell between their tents. "One can scarcely conceive the confusion," Rommel wrote. "It was pitch dark and impossible to see one's hand before one's eyes."

The 90th Light Division entered Mersa Matruh on the morning of June 29, signaling the second impressive victory in a fortnight for Rommel's army. By then, all the enemy soldiers who had not been captured were in full flight eastward. The Germans collected 8,000 prisoners and an immense haul of weapons and supplies. "Now the battle of Mersa Matruh has also been won," Rommel wrote home, "and our leading units are only 125 miles from Alexandria. I think the worst is well behind us."

The furious pace of recent weeks, however, had left many of Rommel's soldiers exhausted. They yearned for the Eden evoked in an entry in the 90th Light's official war diary—"to have a swim in the sea and to sleep one's fill"—but Rommel would permit no letup. It was essential, he believed, to strike before fresh troops and new British and American weapons improved the enemy's chances. He remained confident. On the day his troops occupied Mersa Matruh, he ordered a combat group, the 606th Flak Detachment led by Captain Georg Briel, to advance to Alexandria, stopping only when it reached the suburbs. "When I arrive tomorrow," he told Briel, "we'll drive into Cairo together for a coffee." Briel obediently raced ahead, encountering minimal resistance, until by June 30 he was a scant fifty miles from Alexandria, not far from a little village named El Alamein.

Mussolini, anticipating the imminent conquest of Egypt, flew to North Africa to lead the victory march into Alexandria. Many British civilians in Egypt envisioned the worst. Correspondent Alan Moorehead saw scores of Britons seeking visas to Palestine queued up outside the British consulate. "The Palestine trains were jammed," he wrote. "A thin mist of smoke hung over the British embassy, where huge quantities of secret documents were being burned." The smoke became so thick that the day was known thereafter in the Eighth Army as Ash Wednesday. The British fleet departed Alexandria for Port Said and Haifa.

General Auchinleck ended his withdrawal at El Alamein, a site that British troops had fortified in advance. The defensive line there was a forty-mile-long string of the strongpoints that the British called boxes—complexes of minefields ringed with barbed wire and backed by concrete blockhouses, dugouts, and earthworks. The line stretched south from the blue-green Mediterranean to a row of jagged hills that formed the rim of

Mussolini reviews Italian troops following the capture of Mersa Matruh. Frustrated that the Germans were reaping all the credit in the desert war, the duce flew to the front in late June to share in the anticipated triumphal entry into Alexandria.

the Qattara Depression, a valley 700 feet below sea level that was impassable to heavy vehicles. The El Alamein line could not be outflanked. Rommel would have to drive through it.

When the rest of the army caught up with Briel's group, the Panzerarmee commander was ready with his plan for a new offensive, modeled on the success at Mersa Matruh: The 90th Light, supported by the Italian XIII Corps, would slice through the defenses of the British XXX Corps south of El Alamein and turn north to cut the coast road, blocking the British line of retreat. Farther south, the Afrikakorps and Italian XX Corps were to punch through the center of the line held by the British XIII Corps and play havoc in its rear. The Littorio Division, stiffened by German reconnaissance units, would carry out a feint to the south.

The attack began in darkness early on July 1 *(map, next page)*. Here, as at Mersa Matruh, a hasty reconnaissance had been unable to pinpoint the British strongpoints. The 90th Light tried to skirt the south side of the El Alamein box, at the seaward end of the British line, but strayed into the box's defenses and was pinned down all morning. No sooner did the division get moving again that afternoon, under cover of a dust storm, than it was halted for good by a furious artillery barrage from three South African brigades. Rommel, accompanying the 90th Light, had to lie in the open for two hours during the bombardment. The Light Division was reduced to 58 officers and 1,270 men, and all these survivors could do was dig in.

Attacking farther south, meanwhile, the 15th and 21st Panzer Divisions

Germans in a command car descend the crude road bordering the Qattara Depression *(background)*. Rommel called the arid basin a "fantastic sight," but soft sands made it impassable to vehicles and prevented the Germans from executing their usual flanking maneuver.

Battering at the Gateway to Egypt

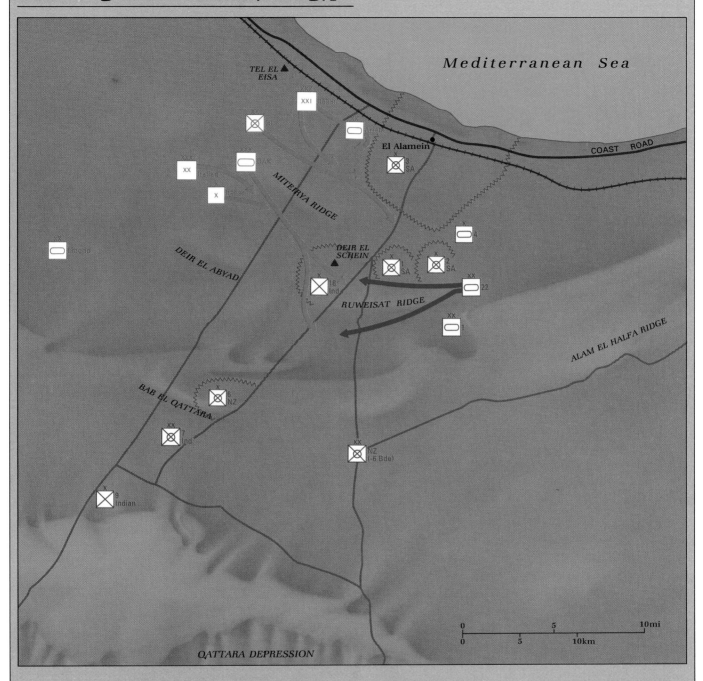

On July 1, 1942, Rommel tried to break through the British line at El Alamein. The 90th Light Division (*red*), advancing on the left, encountered stiff opposition from South African troops (*blue*) dug in near the coast and made little progress. To the south, the 15th and 21st Panzer Divisions—the German Afrikakorps (DAK)—overran the Indian 18th Brigade at Deir el Shein but took heavy losses in the process from enemy air strikes and artillery fire. The next day, Rommel pushed his battered panzers ahead in a fruitless attempt to drive the British from Ruweisat Ridge. Farther to the north, an attempted breakthrough by the Italian Ariete Division was beaten back decisively. Renewed German assaults on July 3 succeeded only in adding to Rommel's steep casualty toll, and that night he broke off the attack.

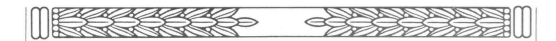

encountered unexpected resistance at the Deir el Shein box and, in savage fighting, annihilated the untried Indian 18th Brigade. But during the exchange, the German tanks were heavily bombed by the RAF and picked off by British antitank guns. By the end of the day, eighteen of fifty-seven panzers had been knocked out.

Rommel knew that his army had lost momentum, but he decided to press on. The next day, he ordered his panzers to renew the attack. Their objective was to seize Ruweisat Ridge, a low, two-mile-long mound of high ground that rose from the desert just east of the Deir el Shein defenses. His panzer divisions made little headway against the tanks and artillery of the entrenched 1st Armored Brigade, which counterattacked, only to be mauled in turn by the Afrikakorps's 88s. To the south, an attempted advance by the Ariete Division was halted and then turned into a route for the Italians. The fighting continued on July 3, but it was obvious that the attackers were not going to break through. British air cover dominated the battlefield. Rommel was immersed in a battle of attrition that he could not win; both his men and his supplies were strained to the breaking point. At nightfall, he instructed his troops to dig in where they were, then signaled Kesselring that he had suspended the attack.

The offensive that had begun on May 26 and had carried Panzerarmee Afrika to the very brink of victory finally halted. For a time, Rommel had appeared to hold Egypt in his grasp, but the moment was now past. "Things are not going as I should like them," he wrote home on July 4. "Resistance is too great, and our strength exhausted."

If the British had launched a strong counterattack at that point, the desert war might have ended then and there. "There is no doubt that we could not have resisted a determined attack by the Eighth Army," Major Mellenthin of Rommel's staff wrote afterward. Auchinleck chose instead to pause and regroup, thus giving the Afrikakorps time to rest and replenish with a trickle of fresh men and supplies, some transported 1,200 miles across the desert from Tripoli. The two sides now faced each other along a static front, a form of warfare Rommel loathed and one that favored his better-equipped foe. German morale did receive a boost from the reappearance of Stukas over Allied lines.

The lull ended when Rommel learned that the British had abandoned the Qaret el Abd box in the southern part of the line. On July 9, he sent the 21st Panzer and the Italian Littorio Divisions to occupy the sector. The puzzling withdrawal from this key position presented him with a new opportunity to sweep into what he perceived as a crumbling British rear. The mystery was cleared up at dawn the next morning, however, when British guns began a bombardment on the seaward end of the front.

General Auchinleck had shifted his operations to the northern sector, hoping to exploit the relatively weak Italian forces stationed there. In the ensuing Allied attack, veteran troops of the Australian 9th Division swarmed out of their dugouts near El Alamein. Striking westward, they overran the Italian Sabratha Division, pursuing its troops along the coast road to the high ground at Tel el Eisa, which the Aussies seized. Fleeing Italian soldiers streamed through the German headquarters, a few miles behind the front, in a flight that Mellenthin described as the "final stages of panic and rout." The Australian attack also cost Rommel his most vital intelligence asset, the Signals Intercept Staff, which had been remarkably successful in monitoring Allied communications. The leader of the eavesdropping unit and most of his men were killed, and their code books and other gear were destroyed.

Mellenthin feared an Allied breakthrough. In the absence of Rommel, who had gone south with his panzers, he cobbled together a rough battle line consisting of headquarters staff and some nearby gun crews. Luckily

Riflemen of the Scots Guard advance behind a screen of tanks at El Alamein in one of the counterthrusts that stymied Rommel's offensive. When the British failed to press their advantage, an officer complained that "the attitude of the Eighth Army was that of having one foot in the stirrup."

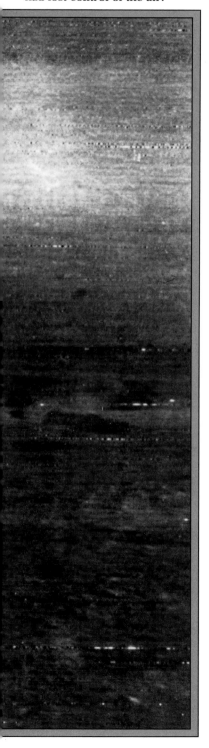

Hit by groundfire during the July fighting, a Stuka crashes in flames near the Egyptian border. By this stage of the desert war, the outnumbered Luftwaffe had lost control of the air.

for the Germans, the lead units of a fresh infantry division, the 164th Light Afrika from Crete, the first major reinforcement the army had received in months, arrived in time to help block the Australian advance. Rommel, meanwhile, hurried north to his headquarters, instructing the panzers to follow. The Australians struck again the following day, mauling another Italian division, the Trieste, south of the coast road. Rommel was becoming more worried about his Italian units—nearly half his army. "We were forced to the conclusion," he wrote, "that the Italians were no longer capable of holding their line."

Seeking as always to regain the offensive, Rommel decided to send the 21st Panzer directly against the El Alamein box. He envisioned a "lightning advance" supported by "every gun and every airplane we could muster," a bold stroke that would reduce the Australian salient if it succeeded. German dive bombers launched the attack on the morning of July 13 with a hard-hitting raid on positions held by South African troops, while Axis artillery pounded the Allied lines. But when the German infantry moved out in a haze of artillery smoke, they were stopped by the enemy's guns before they reached the perimeter wire; the infantrymen had deployed too far in the rear to take quick advantage of the Stuka bombardment.

Rommel attacked again the next day, with the same intent—to sever the Australian salient at Tel el Eisa and reach the sea. But the ground forces again moved too slowly after the air attack, and a combination of El Alamein's guns and the formidable Australian infantry turned them back.

The thrust and parry continued in successive days, the momentum swinging back and forth between the Allies and the Axis. On July 15, Auchinleck turned his attention to the center of the line, to Ruweisat Ridge, hoping again to exploit Rommel's weakest link—the Italians. The New Zealand 2d Division and the Indian 5th Brigade powered through the Italian Brescia and Pavia Divisions holding part of the ridge and threatened to break into the Axis rear. But part of the 15th Panzer Division's 8th Panzer Regiment, passing unnoticed through the Allied lines, mounted a counterattack that night and took 1,200 prisoners to help offset the 2,000 the Italians had lost. The Australians, attacking from their salient on the sea, hammered the Italians again on July 16 and 17. Only massive Afrikakorps artillery bombardments halted the overwhelming enemy advance. Rommel was forced to attach German forces to the Italian units as "corset stays" to stiffen their resistance.

The arrival of Kesselring and the Italian commander, Field Marshal Ugo Cavallero, at Rommel's headquarters on July 17 gave the Desert Fox a chance to plead again for the supplies—especially gasoline—that he desperately needed. A stormy meeting ended in Cavallero's promise of help,

but Rommel's experience with the Italian supply operations made him skeptical. Words of frustration and even despair began to appear in his letters home. "The enemy is using his superiority to destroy the Italian formations one by one," he wrote that night, "and the German formations are much too weak to stand alone. It's enough to make one weep." A day later he wrote, "There's help in sight, but whether we will live to see it is questionable." Mussolini, his triumphant entry into Alexandria now postponed indefinitely, gave up the wait and returned to Italy.

A four-day break in the action ended on July 21, when Auchinleck again attacked at the center of the front. Waves of New Zealand and Indian infantry penetrated Axis lines on Ruweisat Ridge that night, then waited for armored support that never arrived. The New Zealanders took the brunt of the successful German counterattack that followed, losing more than 1,000 men and 25 artillery pieces. The British 23d Armored Brigade, newly arrived from England, was ordered to drive a wedge between the defenders but was sent to the wrong place because of a communications mix-up. As

Fire from an RAF fighter homes in on an enemy locomotive on the Tobruk-to-El Daba railway. Rommel harbored "tremendous hopes" that the railroad, originally laid by the British, would ease his dire supply situation, but a shortage of rolling stock and RAF vigilance rendered the line almost useless.

a result, the hapless newcomers ended up in a minefield, under fire from German antitank guns. Then the 21st Panzer launched a ferocious counterattack that finished off the brigade. Rommel's defensive might was succeeding where his offense had failed; that day, the Germans took more than 1,400 prisoners and destroyed some 100 British tanks.

Auchinleck tried again on July 26, with similarly dismal results. The Australians drove south and breached the German lines but fell back after tank support again failed to materialize. This time, the British armored commander held back his tanks because he considered the gaps that the infantry had cleared in the minefield to be inadequate. The British infantry marched on alone and was mauled. The Allies lost 1,000 more men and 40 more tanks. Rommel's mood was brightening. "The worst of our troubles are disappearing," he wrote home.

The Eighth Army had suffered 13,000 casualties during the seesaw fight-

A British soldier inspects the remains of an Axis supply caravan hit by a coordinated air and ground assault—one of many raids that plagued the Panzerarmee Afrika in the summer of 1942. Rommel's operations chief warned that, in the competition to keep front-line troops supplied, "our enemies were gaining a decisive lead."

ing in July. German losses also were high, and Rommel was less able to afford them. It was Auchinleck, however, who now broke off the fighting. He had "reluctantly concluded," he said in a message to superiors in London, that further offensives against the Panzerarmee were not presently feasible. He needed fresh and better-trained men. His army would be ready again, he estimated, by mid-September.

Churchill flew to Cairo three days after receiving Auchinleck's bleak report. The general had succeeded in holding Rommel at bay, but this was not enough for Churchill. The string of defeats in the desert had brought the morale of the British public to low ebb and even threatened Churchill's political future. Following Tobruk, the prime minister had faced a censure vote in the House of Commons on his conduct of the war. He won handily, but the situation in the desert remained precarious. Churchill—and Britain—needed a victory, and it no longer seemed that Auchinleck was the man to provide one. Again, Churchill made changes at the top. He appointed General Sir Harold Alexander as commander in chief, Middle East, and General W. H. E. Gott as commander of the Eighth Army. Gott never made it to the front, however. As his transport headed toward Cairo on August 7, Luftwaffe fighters forced it down, and the general was killed as he helped rescue the wounded. As a result, command of the Eighth Army devolved on a relatively obscure officer, Lieut. General Bernard Law Montgomery. Although he was slated for senior command in the planned Allied invasion of Tunisia, Montgomery's most recent assignment had been a training command in England.

Montgomery promised no more withdrawals, a resolute stand at the El Alamein line, and an attack when he was good and ready. Churchill told him that his "foremost duty" was to destroy or capture Rommel's army. August, meanwhile, brought a welcome, month-long respite for the exhausted troops, who peered at each other across a heat-hazed desert littered with minefields. The contending armies occupied themselves with what Rommel called a "race to reorganize." But the Germans were losing from the start. In hindsight, it was now apparent that Kesselring had been right and Rommel wrong in their argument about whether to invade Malta in June. RAF bombers based on Malta, together with British warships, were mercilessly pounding Axis supply convoys, and their marksmanship was improving: Six Axis ships had been sunk in June, seven in July, and twelve in August. Precious quantities of fuel and ammunition had gone down with them. The Germans were also losing the supply war along the African coast, where RAF raiders strafed trucks and boats ferrying cargo between German-held ports and the Axis lines; three coastal vessels were sent to the bottom in a single day.

Prime Minister Churchill, wearing a pith helmet during a flying visit to Egypt in mid-August, confers with *(from left)* General Harold Alexander, Middle East commander in chief; General Bernard Montgomery, Eighth Army commander; and General Alan Brooke, chief of the Imperial General Staff.

Rommel fumed about the resultant shortfall. In early August, the supplies that reached his army barely covered its daily needs. New units arrived without vehicles, which put a greater strain on the already overextended transport columns. Rommel was forced to ban harassing fire to save ammunition. He complained that the Italian supply command made sure that rear-echelon Italian units were adequately equipped while frontline Axis outfits went lacking, their trucks and guns collecting dust at depots in Italy. In mid-August, he reported to Berlin that he was 50 percent below strength in armor, 40 percent in antitank guns, 30 percent in artillery ammunition, and 25 percent—16,000 men—below his troop requirements.

Rommel and others in the German high command suspected that the Allies' extraordinary success in pinpointing and sinking Axis shipping was more than good luck. Postwar revelations showed that they were right. Once again, Ultra decodings and local message intercepts by the Royal Navy enabled the British fleet to locate the convoys. As a cover, British intelligence put out a tale that a circle of high-ranking Italian naval officers, sympathetic to the Allied cause, regularly passed to the British information indicating the sailing times and routes of the Axis Mediterranean convoys.

A surprising quantity of men and supplies nonetheless got through. In late August, the Afrikakorps was bolstered by the addition of 203 new tanks—including 73 Panzer III models, with powerful 50-mm guns, and 27 Panzer IVs, armed with the latest long-barreled 75-mm gun. Fresh troops brought the tattered 15th and 21st Panzer close to normal strength, but

gasoline remained the army's most severe problem. Meeting with Kessel-ring and Cavallero on August 27, Rommel demanded a minimum of 6,000 tons of fuel for the new offensive he was planning. "You can start your battle, Field Marshal," Cavallero replied confidently; tankers were on the way. Ultimately, only a fraction of this fuel reached the army. The British destroyed four tankers in the last few days of August, and much of the rest was consumed by the trucks hauling it to the front. The Allied army, meanwhile, was regularly being resupplied under RAF cover.

The fifty-year-old Rommel was simultaneously coping with weakness from an unexpected quarter—his own body. His nineteen-month-long stint in North Africa was beginning to grind him down. No other German officer past the age of forty had lasted that long. There were days when he could barely get up. He suffered from a severe nasal infection and, perhaps, chronic gastritis. Fainting spells and low blood pressure compounded his misery. His doctor pronounced him unfit to command in combat and recommended a long sick leave. Rommel, reluctantly agreeing, suggested that General Heinz Guderian replace him, but when Guderian, who had fallen out of favor with the Führer, was rejected by Berlin, Rommel decided to stay on and launch the attack that he considered crucial.

"Today," began his order of the day for August 30, "the army, strength-ened by new divisions, is embarking on the final destruction of the enemy in a renewed attack. I expect every soldier under my command during these decisive hours to give his utmost." For Rommel, the constant ag-gressor, the innovator, and the high-stakes risktaker, it was now or never. This battle would decide who controlled North Africa. "It will be a long time," he wrote to Lucie, "before we get such favorable conditions of moonlight, relative strengths, etc., again." The moon would be full, illu-minating the battlefield. He had 500 tanks to the enemy's 700, and some 146,000 men in all to Montgomery's 177,000. At least 80 percent of his trucks had been captured from the enemy, however, creating a spare-parts night-mare for the overworked combat repair crews.

The Desert Fox was gambling that fuel would be delivered as promised and that British air superiority—which his staff overestimated at five to one—would not prove decisive. When he left his sleeping truck on the day of the assault, he told his doctor that the decision to attack was "the hardest I have ever taken. Either the army in Russia succeeds in getting through to Grozny and we in Africa manage to reach the Suez Canal or. . . ." He finished the sentence with a gesture signifying defeat.

His tactical plan again depended on speed and surprise to offset the enemy's numerical advantages; quick maneuvers would compensate for relative weakness. The plan called for the newly arrived 164th Light Afrika

Heroics to Keep the Army Running

Suffering steady losses of tanks and other vehicles and starved for replacements, the Afrikakorps would have frozen in place but for the herculean efforts of its mobile repair crews. The repairmen routinely set up shop close behind the front and went forward in massive recovery vehicles to bring back damaged tanks—often while the battle raged.

The mechanics, metalworkers, electricians, and other specialists became remarkably adept at improvising repairs. They restored shell-torn and worn-out vehicles virtually from the ground up, using parts cannibalized from German or even captured British equipment. Working in 120-degree heat and exposed to enemy artillery fire, they overhauled engines, repaired transmissions, rewired electrical systems, and, when they had to, machined new parts on portable lathes.

British repair facilities stayed far to the rear. As a result, British armor that broke down in the desert was usually written off. By contrast, scores of banged-up German vehicles returned to duty. This internal resupply was in fact Rommel's ace in the hole, saving his finite desert fleet to fight again another day.

Using a portable hoist, mechanics at a panzer division's front-line repair shop lift the engine from a disabled reconnaissance car.

A mechanic, working stripped to the waist, inserts a new metal leaf into a rebuilt leaf spring.

Checking his work, one member of a repair team revs up the engine of an ambulance. Two others sit on the fenders, listening to determine whether the repaired engine sounds in tune.

An electrician fills batteries with distilled water while his mates fix a motorcycle outside a makeshift supply shop. The desert heat was so ferocious that mechanics buried spare wheels in the relatively cool sand to keep the rims from warping.

Working from a large, derrick-equipped truck, a repair team installs a refurbished turret in an armored scout car without leaving the battlefront.

Division and the Ramcke Paratroop Brigade, along with Italian troops, to pin down the British on the north and center, while the Afrikakorps attacked far to the south, near the Qattara Depression, and turned the British left flank. The panzer divisions would then wheel northward in a drive to capture Alam Halfa Ridge, a key topographical feature deep in the rear of the Eighth Army.

Rommel was banking on a slow reaction by the British commanders and also hoping that a clever ruse would mislead them. He had ordered camouflage cover for the tanks and artillery positions on both the northern and central sectors of the front line. But on the south, where the attack would come, he deployed dummy tanks built in a way that enabled the enemy, by close observation, to recognize them as fake. This bit of deviousness would presumably lead them to expect the main assault elsewhere.

The force began moving forward in bright moonlight at eleven o'clock on August 30. The 90th Light Division was to the south of the Italian X Corps, which formed the pivot point of a broad Axis front. The Italian XX Corps advanced in the middle, the Afrikakorps on the right. Two small detachments, the 3d and 33d Reconnaissance, covered the extreme right along the Qattara Depression. It was soon apparent that Rommel's ruse had fooled no one *(map, page 159)*. British intelligence knew from monitoring his radio traffic where the main thrust was coming, and Montgomery had reinforced that sector. The attacking troops ran into trouble immediately. They had to cover thirty miles of desert before beginning their attack, and much of the area was known to be mined. They encountered minefields deeper and thicker than expected. British armor, artillery, and machine guns inflicted heavy losses on the mine-clearing teams and the men pinned behind them. German tanks awaiting removal of the mines were illuminated by RAF magnesium flares and bombed, the first sign that Allied air superiority would play a major role in the battle.

Rommel's timetable, which relied on speed, was already out of kilter. The troops who were supposed to wheel north after dawn were still mired in the minefields when the sun rose. Now three key German commanders fell: Lieut. General Walther Nehring, the Afrikakorps commander, was seriously wounded, and several members of his staff killed, when his vehicle was bombed by an RAF plane; the 21st Panzer commander, Major General Georg von Bismarck, was killed by a mine; and Major General Ulrich Kleemann of the 90th Light was seriously wounded. Rommel considered calling off the attack, but when he learned at about half past eight that Afrikakorps tanks had finally broken through the minefield and were moving east, he decided to continue.

The desert heat was scorching by this time, despite low clouds, and a

dry southerly wind spawned a sandstorm that swept across the battlefield. The Afrikakorps slogged ahead, hampered by the storm and later by soft sand that slowed the tanks further and increased their consumption of gasoline. Worse for Rommel, the new stocks of fuel had not appeared.

Not until the evening of August 31 did the German armored units reach Alam Halfa. Having anticipated German intentions, the British had bolstered the defenses of the ridge until it fairly bristled with firepower. Some 400 tanks had been massed there, and the British 2d Armored had concealed its heavy Grants behind sand dunes and dug them in. Artillery crews had rehearsed for weeks, sprinting to their positions in darkness, in anticipation of the moment now approaching. Their new six-pounder antitank guns were to remain silent until the foe was within 400 yards. The German troops attacked the entrenched British positions after nightfall, destroying dozens of Grant tanks but incurring heavy casualties. Losses were high on both sides, but the defenders held on. The Germans dug in where they were and endured a nightlong pounding from RAF bombers.

On the morning of September 1, Rommel was so short of gasoline that he had to limit the attack on the ridge to the 15th Panzer. The assault withered under a tremendous bombardment from Allied guns and planes. The rain of fire and steel kept German tanks and infantry immobilized for the rest of the day. Because his tanks were now nearly out of fuel, Rommel knew that his army was stopped, and it was becoming increasingly clear that its survival was at stake. On September 2, Rommel decided to retreat, but the shortage of fuel precluded even a large-scale withdrawal; men and tanks would have to retreat piecemeal.

Rommel himself, still very sick, came under aerial attack six times that morning as he toured Afrikakorps positions. Once, he barely made it to a trench, where, a few inches away, he saw a spade "pierced clean through" by a red-hot metal splinter that landed beside him.

The next day, Rommel's troops began gradually pulling back. By September 6, most had settled into their former positions. In the south, they retained some of the British minefields, adding them to their own, but that was small consolation. The balance of losses in the battle—which German soldiers called the six-day race, after a famous German bicycle race—was lopsidedly in the Allies' favor: Rommel estimated his casualties at 3,000. His retreating army had to abandon 50 tanks, 50 antitank and field guns, and about 400 other vehicles. Alexander counted British losses at 1,640 men, 68 tanks, and 18 antitank guns.

Montgomery's debut as Eighth Army commander had been a defensive success, but his failure to follow up with a full-scale counterattack mystified many, including Rommel's aide Mellenthin. Acknowledging that the

British commander "forfeited an excellent opportunity" to destroy the Panzerarmee, Mellenthin speculated the most likely explanation was his chief's reputation, especially his "well-known brilliance in counterattack."

The German command suffered no illusions about the significance of the battle of Alam Halfa. "With the failure of this offensive, our last chance of gaining the Suez Canal had gone," Rommel wrote. He cited three reasons for the outcome: British strength at his point of attack, "contrary to our reconnaissance reports"; RAF domination of the air; and the shortage of fuel. By the evening of September 1, his army had had sufficient fuel for only one day's action; three Axis tankers had been sunk between September 2 and 4 while only one had reached Tobruk. Other German soldiers offered less statistical explanations for the defeat. Lieutenant Heinz Schmidt thought that "our panzers had literally lost their spirit." Field Marshal Kesselring believed that the "old Rommel" would have won this battle; the "iron determination to persevere was lacking."

Rommel found himself in an unaccustomed role—digging in on a defensive line and yielding the initiative. His engineers created a network of minefields he called the Devil's Gardens. In September and October, nearly 500,000 mines were laid along the forty-mile front in fields as deep as five miles. The mines were sometimes planted in layers to confound the British sappers: If the mine on top was found and removed, the one beneath it would explode. Grenades and artillery shells were buried and rigged to tripwires. Behind the minefields, Rommel deployed his troops—infantry first, then artillery and antitank crews, and finally armor.

For the German soldiers on the front lines, September brought the first real rest in four months. Seeking ways to keep the men occupied, Rommel's command organized refresher courses, band concerts, and a medley of other entertainment. Twelve speakers able to talk amusingly on a variety of subjects were available. The 104th Panzer Grenadiers organized a comedy troupe that proved especially popular. Ceremonies celebrated obscure milestones, such as the 155th Artillery Regiment's 80,000th round fired and the four millionth loaf of bread baked by 15th Panzer's bakers.

Midway through September, Rommel yielded to his doctor's orders and agreed to go home on medical leave for treatment of his various ailments. He told his replacement, General Georg Stumme, that he would hasten back in the event of a British offensive. Then he flew to Italy on September 23 for a meeting with Mussolini. The duce, listening with little interest to his complaints about supplies and Allied air supremacy, thought Rommel seemed "physically and morally shaken." Three days later, Rommel aired the same grievances at Hitler's East Prussian headquarters, where the mood struck him as oddly optimistic.

The Do-or-Die Charge of the Panzers

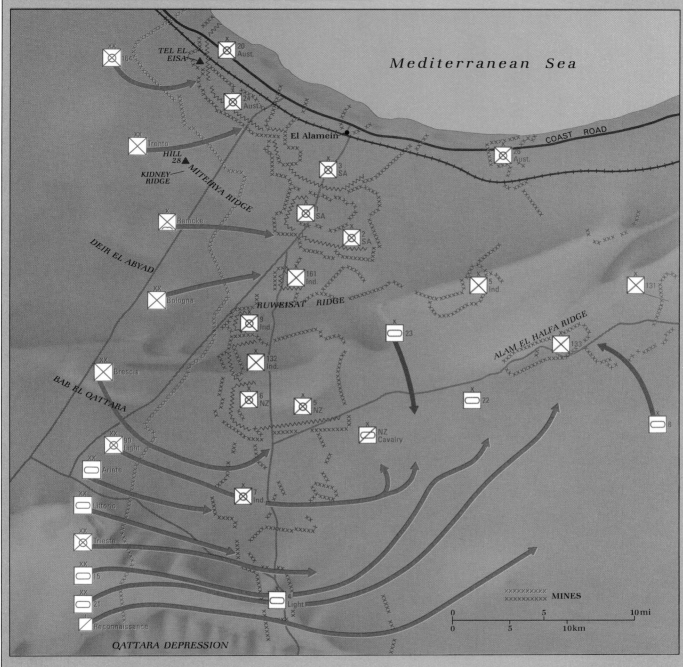

On August 30, Rommel launched his climactic effort to crush the British Eighth Army and reach Alexandria. As at Gazala in May, his plan called for an armored sweep around the southern flank while infantry preoccupied the enemy to the north. But the British were ready for the end run and blasted the panzers from the air and ground as they crossed the minefields above the Qattara Depression. Elements of the 15th and 21st Panzer made it through on August 31 and swung north toward their objective—Alam Halfa Ridge—but they were short on fuel and outmatched by the British tanks and guns on the ridge. After costly attempts to force the enemy from the high ground, on September 2 Rommel began to withdraw his forces to their original position.

The Führer presented him with a field marshal's baton and promised help—new tanks and cargo vessels, ammunition, even rocket launchers. Rommel spelled out his supply demands in tonnage: at least 30,000 tons in September and 35,000 in October. His description of a new American-made armor-piercing shell, used by Allied warplanes against his panzers with devastating effectiveness, precipitated a tense exchange with Hermann Göring. "That's impossible!" the Luftwaffe commander declared. "The Americans only know how to make razor blades." Rommel replied, "We could do with some of those razor blades, Herr Reich Marshal." Later, at a Berlin press conference arranged by Joseph Goebbels, the minister of propaganda, Rommel tried to convey an optimism he did not feel. Then, early in October, he and his wife settled in for a period of rest at Semmering, an Austrian mountain resort.

As Rommel regained his strength, his army awaited the inevitable Allied ground offensive. The Allied advantage in air power that Rommel bemoaned became increasingly apparent. RAF bomber squadrons, flying in tidy formations that German soldiers called "party rallies" because of their resemblance to flybys at prewar Nazi rallies, hounded the Panzerarmee almost daily in September and October. On October 9 alone, RAF raiders flew 500 sorties; the Luftwaffe, hampered by a shortage of fuel, could muster only 102. Nerves grew raw under the pounding. One artillery corporal wore a placard on his back that read, "No whistling." An eye cocked skyward became known as a "German glance." In late October, the comparative

Toiling in the Devil's Gardens, the defensive cordon established in September, German engineers *(above)* plant antitank mines at irregular distances. No longer strong enough to attack, the Axis forces installed 445,358 mines and strung miles of barbed wire *(right)* to thwart Montgomery's expected onslaught.

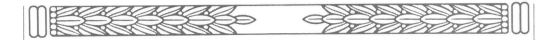

strength in the air stood at 605 fighters and 315 bombers for the British against 347 fighters and 243 bombers for the Germans. Rommel acknowledged that "there was no real answer to the enemy's air superiority."

The infantrymen behind the Devil's Gardens, meanwhile, were still short of everything. They needed tanks, guns, ammunition, trucks, food, and, of course, fuel. Rommel had reported before going on leave that, without sufficient supplies, "the continued successful maintenance of the African theater of war will be impossible." Less than half of Rommel's minimum fuel requirements for September and October were shipped. Now his men were on short rations because only half their food had been delivered. Poor nutrition was causing cases of hepatitis and dysentery. One food shipment was cut back so the space could be used for weapons. "We stop one hole," General Stumme exclaimed, "only to tear another hole open."

The slender allotments that did arrive—the two panzer divisions grew to about 100 tanks each in the month of October—were far short of the stockpiles Montgomery was accumulating. Having received shipments of such weapons as American-made Sherman tanks, six-pounder antitank guns, and self-propelled, 105-mm howitzers, the Eighth Army was now superior in both the quality and the quantity of its armaments. Montgom-

Escorted by Propaganda Minister Joseph Goebbels *(right),* **Rommel arrives at a Nazi rally in Berlin carrying the field marshal's baton**

that Hitler presented him a few days earlier. "I had rather," Rommel wrote, "that he had given me one more division."

ery spent the September-October hiatus assembling a juggernaut and training his men. By mid-October, he had an edge of roughly two to one or better across the board: 194,000 men to 104,000 Axis troops, 1,000 tanks to 500, and 908 field guns to 299.

Montgomery chose the night of October 23 to launch his assault. A full moon would again light the way for the attackers. He had devised an elaborate plan *(map, page 173)*. Under the cover of a massive artillery bombardment, four infantry divisions of Lieut. General Oliver Leese's XXX Corps would attack in the north on a six-mile front stretching south from the hill called Tel el Eisa, on the sea, to Miteirya Ridge. The infantry and its sappers would clear lanes through the minefields and eradicate German infantry positions and machine-gun emplacements. Then the tanks of Lieut. General Herbert Lumsden's X Corps would roll forward to smash Axis defenses. In the south, Lieut. General Brian Horrock's XIII Corps would launch a diversionary attack to occupy the panzers in that sector and further confuse the Germans as to the Eighth Army's true objective. Allied warplanes would bomb German positions and attack forward Axis airfields to keep enemy aircraft from playing a role in the defense.

The British commander also designed a Rommel-like ploy to convince the Germans that the main attack would come in the south. To deceive Axis air reconnaissance, the British erected three and a half dummy field regiments of heavy artillery and manned the guns with phony gunners. Allied soldiers also began to build a dummy water pipeline, complete with pumping stations, out of old gasoline cans. The line ran twenty miles south to a portion of desert dotted with stacks of dummy supplies. The unfinished construction was calculated to suggest to the Germans that the attack would not come until the pipeline was completed. Tanks and guns behind the real jumping-off point in the north were disguised as trucks.

The night of October 23 proved to be so bright that men trying to sleep in the rear areas had to pull the covers over their heads to keep out the moonlight. The assault began at 9:30 p.m. with an earth-shaking artillery barrage—the biggest since World War I. Nine hundred British guns fired roughly 300 rounds each in a hurricane of fire that lasted twenty minutes. On the six-mile-wide invasion front, the guns were spaced an average of one every twenty-one yards. When the infantry moved out, the artillerymen shifted their aim forward to provide a moving curtain of fire ahead of the troops. Unnerved by the barrage, many Italian soldiers of the Littorio Division bolted from forward positions and fled toward the rear. The British, Australian, New Zealand, and South African units in the Allied vanguard quickly overran the remaining Axis outposts.

By dawn, however, the Allied infantry's advance had slowed to a crawl

Luftwaffe ace Hans-Joachim Marseille flashes a winner's smile as a crew member paints a fiftieth victory bar on his Me 109.

An Affable Ace of Aces

The most celebrated fighting man in Libya, barring only Rommel, was a youthful aviator named Hans-Joachim Marseille, acclaimed by the German press as the African Eagle. Berlin-born but of French descent, Marseille was a fearsome killer in the air—and a charming bon vivant on the ground. He contrived to invent amusing pranks on the dustiest desert airfields, and his tent, renowned for its well-stocked bar, had the raffish air of a Paris café. Marseille was a pilot of uncommon skill, pushing his Messerschmitt into tight turns and daring climbs that leveled off only at the point of stalling. He was most of all a lethal marksman, able to hit an RAF opponent with a short burst while both aircraft were flashing through the sky at top speed.

Even for the Luftwaffe, where it was customary in dogfights to defer to the squadron's aces, Marseille's totals were astounding: He flew 388 sorties and destroyed 158 enemy planes. And on a single day at the battle of Alam Halfa, he shot down 17 planes. Yet even Marseille's good fortune could not last.

Marseille (*above*) settles into the cockpit of his Messerschmitt fighter. Unmilitary in style, he preferred shorts to flight suits, and he often wore sneakers, which he said gave him a more sensitive touch on the pedals.

Employing the universal language of the fighter pilot, Marseille (*center*) uses his hands to describe the dogfight that resulted in his fiftieth kill on April 1, 1942. His victory string was abetted by the agility of his Me 109, which outclassed most of the RAF aircraft in Africa.

Perusing his press notices in a Libyan village, Marseille reads a poster on a makeshift kiosk announcing that he has won the oak leaves to the Iron Cross he wears around his neck.

Photos of German movie stars adorn one wall of Marseille's tent, and a flowered quilt from home decorates the other. In a typically youthful touch, he has tacked to the ceiling a fake spider web that is inhabited by a menacing toy spider.

Returning from a mission over Cairo on September 30, 1942, Marseille radioed his base, "There is smoke in my cockpit!" The Messerschmitt's engine was on fire. Marseille bailed out, but he struck the plane's tail and apparently was knocked unconscious. His chute never opened. The Germans recovered his body in the desert and accorded him a hero's funeral (above). General Adolf Galland, the Luftwaffe's chief fighter pilot, called the young Marseille an "unrivaled virtuoso." He had died two months short of only his twenty-third birthday.

through the Devil's Gardens. A few units had reached their objectives, but only one tank corridor had been cleared. Stubborn defensive fire and local counterattacks by elements of the fresh 164th Light Afrika held the line. Divisional artillery of the 443d Battalion had to fire over open sights to seal off one breakthrough attempt. General Stumme, meanwhile, knew little about the battle. His communications with the front had been shattered by the opening barrage, and he determined to drive up to get a firsthand look. With one staff officer and a driver, he set off for the battlefront early in the morning. Near the front, his command car came under fire from Australian machine gunners. The staff officer slumped in his seat, fatally wounded. As the driver swung around at high speed, Stumme was stricken by a fatal heart attack, and he tumbled out of the vehicle, unnoticed by the terrified driver. Stumme was later reported missing, but not killed in action. His unexplained absence threw the German command into confusion.

Heavy fighting persisted all day and through the night as the men of the Littorio Division and the 15th Panzer tried to stem the British pressure on a key elevated point that the Germans designated Hill 28. The hill dominated its sector of the battlefield even though it was only twenty feet higher than the surrounding desert terrain. As the Axis line stiffened, casualties mounted on both sides. Tank divisions squared off against each other, and in two days about 250 Allied tanks were lost, as well as 88 of 119 for the 15th Panzer. The ever-present RAF rained bombs on Axis positions. General Ritter von Thoma, who had only recently taken over the Afrikakorps, replaced Stumme in overall command.

Rommel learned of the attack by telephone on the afternoon of October 24. He was told that Stumme was missing and was asked if he was well enough to return. Rommel said he was. Hitler called a few hours later and asked if he could start at once. Rommel left early the next day, stopped at Rome, and reached his headquarters at sundown. In Rome, he had learned that his army was still short of fuel. He knew then, as he wrote later, that "there were no more laurels to be earned in Africa"—at least for him.

Montgomery broke off the diversionary attack on the south edge of the line, in front of his bogus pipeline, on October 25. That night, the Australian 9th Division, operating near the coast at the other end of the front, seized Hill 28—the Aussies called it Kidney Ridge for its kidney-bean shape. They prevailed in bitter hand-to-hand skirmishing after learning from a captured map the disposition of Axis troops and mines in the area. Rommel rounded up part of the 90th Light Division and his own headquarter's defense troops to back up Axis armor and managed to prevent further breakthroughs, but the cost in men and machines was becoming disastrous for the Germans, especially for the battered 15th Panzer.

The field marshal was convinced that his opponents, using his own tactics against him, were seeking a breakthrough point. And as he listened to Thoma and other officers brief him after his return, he also realized that his options were starkly limited. The fuel shortage made a major move impossible. All he could do was try to hurl the Australians back from the salient they had established near the coast. Rommel watched as "load after load of bombs cascaded down among my troops." The Allied firepower was overwhelming. Nor would there be any immediate relief for the fuel crisis: Wellington bombers sank two more Axis supply ships that day off Benghazi.

Belatedly, Rommel began to concentrate his armor and other mobile forces. He brought the 90th Light Division up to the line from its position in reserve and moved the 21st Panzer from the south to the coast, even though not enough fuel remained to get the division back south, if necessary. He ordered the 21st to counterattack north of Miteirya Ridge on October 27. Once more, Axis forces lunged at the ridge, but unimpeded RAF bombers combined with ferocious fire from Allied antitank guns to stifle the infantry and tank assault after a brutal melee. Panzer losses included thirty-seven more tanks. Now the Germans had only eighty-one left.

The tone of Rommel's notes home turned increasingly despondent. "Dearest Lu," he wrote on October 28, "Who knows whether I'll have a chance to sit down in peace in the next few days or ever again? Today there's still a chance." The next day he wrote, "I haven't much hope left." He was even gloomier in his account of the October 27 counterattack: "It is obvious that from now on the British will destroy us bit by bit." More chilling still was his observation that, "as yet, Montgomery has thrown only half his striking force into the battle." Rommel remained puzzled that the British commander had not attempted to break through.

Despite the odds and his steadily weakening position—or perhaps because of it—Rommel was still inclined to attack. When infantry of the Australian 9th and an armored force broke through German lines near the coast road on October 31, he led the successful counterattack himself with the 33d Reconnaissance, calling up the last of his Stukas and sealing the breach with remnants of the 21st and 15th Panzer Divisions. This brought a congratulatory message from Cavallero, who cited Mussolini's "complete confidence" that Rommel would yet prevail. The high command, Rommel realized, failed to understand his predicament.

Montgomery also had cause for concern. His assault had been designed to lure the German armored forces to their destruction against his antitank and artillery superiority, but four days into the battle, most of his forces were short of the objectives planned for the first day and the Panzerarmee Afrika was obviously not broken. To make matters worse, his own armored

During the Eighth Army's decisive push, launched on October 23, British troops pass a slain gunner, who hangs from the turret of a Panzer III. After ten days, Rommel lost hope of stemming the tide: "We are simply being crushed by the enemy's weight."

formations were still not free to maneuver. The British commander feared that if a stalemate continued, his soldiers might lose their momentum and their morale. Still husbanding reserves of both infantry and armor, Montgomery prepared to launch an all-out assault, which he code-named Operation Supercharge. At first, he intended to mass his forces in the north to exploit the gains of the Australian division. But when British intelligence reported that all Rommel's German divisions were now concentrated in that area, leaving Italian infantry to hold most of the front line, Montgomery shifted his point of attack. The Australians would continue to hammer westward along the coast, but the new effort would come five miles farther south, aimed at the juncture between the 164th Light Afrika and the Italian

Trentino Division. Behind them lay a juncture between the 15th Panzer and the Littorio Division.

At one o'clock on November 2, the night exploded with the flash and thunder of another stupendous artillery barrage. In the prelude to Operation Supercharge, all the artillery of the British XXX Corps, 360 guns, ignited the darkness, hurling 15,000 shells into the narrow 4,000-yard front. For four hours, shells rained on the Axis positions while relays of bombers pounded the thin Axis ranks. Allied infantry, led by men of the crack New Zealand 2d Division, plodded forward, with tanks right behind them. By four o'clock, the infantry had gained four miles of desert and cleared the last of the Devil's Gardens. As planned, armored cars of the 9th Armored Brigade passed through the infantry and headed for the Axis rear areas. They were followed by tanks of three armored divisions.

The British tanks soon encountered opposition. Rommel, alerted to British intentions by the preliminary bombardment, had time to establish a lethal screen of antitank and field guns behind a road called the Rahman Track. Tanks of the 15th Panzer Division took hull-down positions in support of the gunners. By now, the sky was beginning to lighten in the east behind the attacking British tanks, giving the German gunners starkly silhouetted targets. As their rounds hit home, tanks erupted in flames and smoke, and crewmen dived out of hatches to save themselves. Not many of the tanks made it across the track; those that did, however, raised brutal havoc among the defending gun crews, crushing the German gunners beneath their treads or spraying them with machine-gun fire. Some German troops attacked the tanks singlehandedly. Lieutenant Ralf Ringler of the 104th Panzer Grenadiers tossed a grenade at the turret of a British tank and saw it bounce off. He was close enough to hear the British tank commander exclaim, "Near miss!"

The toll swiftly mounted on both sides. Within an hour, the British had lost seventy tanks. Two brigades of the 1st Armored Division moved up to reinforce the remnants of the 9th Armored. On the German side, Rommel and Thoma counterattacked, ordering what was left of the 15th and 21st Panzer Divisions to stop the British advance by hitting hard from both sides. All available 88-mm guns were wheeled into action. In the swirling tank battle that ensued, the Shermans, Grants, and Crusaders dueled at point-blank range with the Panzer IIIs and IVs that had so long been the steel at the core of Rommel's army. The Germans stubbornly held the key to the battlefield, a ridge called Tel el Aqqaqir. The RAF staged nonstop raids on German gun emplacements concentrated around the battle area. Rommel watched from a little hill as the squadrons of British- and American-made bombers knocked out one precious 88 after another.

A Vain Effort to Hold the Line

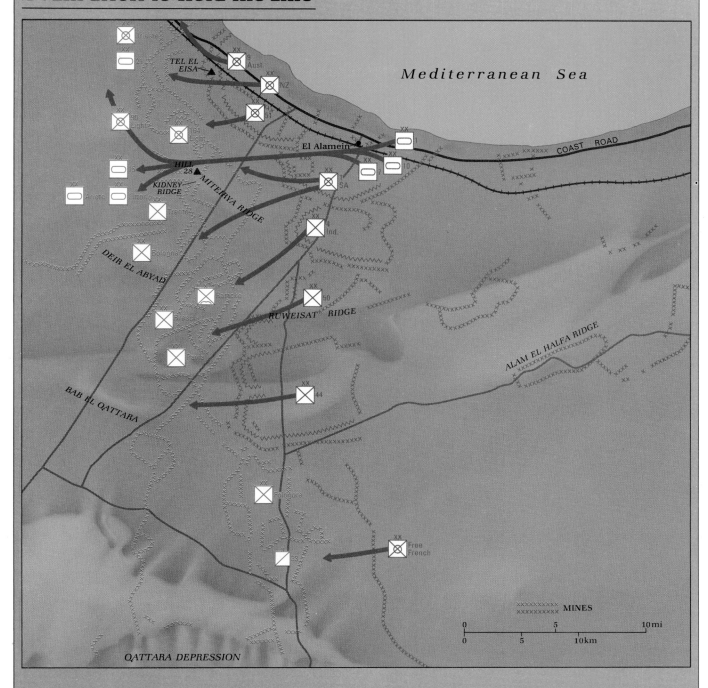

By October 23, the British were ready to bring their numerically superior forces to bear against Rommel's ill-equipped army. That night, a massive artillery barrage paved the way for British infantry to begin slowly clearing tank corridors through dense German minefields at the northern end of the line. In response, the 15th Panzer Division moved to counter the threat in conjunction with the 90th Light, leading to desperate fighting around Kidney Ridge on October 26 and 27. The Germans held the line, but their best units were wearing down. Rommel, who had rushed to the front from Germany after the battle began, concentrated what was left of his armor in the north, leaving a vulnerable area to the south that the British exploited in a second concerted drive on November 2. By November 4, Rommel's shattered army was in full retreat.

As night fell, the battle still raged, and Thoma briefed Rommel on the situation. The Germans had sealed off the Allied breakthrough, but the Afrikakorps was left with only 35 tanks. The number of German guns—including the 88s—had been reduced by two-thirds during the battle. No German reserves were left, and the 100 or so Italian tanks still in operation had proved useless in battle. Rommel had no choice. That night, he ordered Thoma to prepare a withdrawal to a defensive position at Fuka, sixty miles west, and signaled Berlin that he was retreating. Sporadic fighting continued through the night, but on the morning of November 3, silence prevailed. Rommel sent an aide to explain his army's plight to Hitler in person, but the Führer had already decided differently. Rommel received the message in the early afternoon. "In the situation in which you find yourself," Hitler's order read, "there can be no other thought but to stand fast. It would not be the first time in history that a strong will has triumphed over the bigger battalions. As to your troops, you can show them no other road than that to victory or death."

Hitler's order stunned Rommel. He radioed Berlin that his losses among infantry, antitank, and engineer detachments were nearly 50 percent and that two Italian armored divisions, the Ariete and Littorio, had been all but wiped out. His position was hopeless. Still, he could not bring himself to disobey Hitler's direct order. In what he described as a "kind of apathy," he instructed all units to hold fast.

The shredded ranks of underfed and outnumbered but tenacious troops obeyed one more time, but they, too, recognized the futility of their effort. "We are here, a few grenadiers in our foxholes," a lieutenant in the 104th Panzer Grenadiers wrote in his diary on November 3. "The cold has passed, but hunger remains. Every twenty yards and, in places, at about fifty, lie a few men. Two antitank guns, that is all. And facing us, an armada of tanks."

Doggedly, the remnants of the Afrikakorps delayed the British armored thrust through the morning of November 4. General Thoma, leading his men at the front, was taken prisoner. The Italian Bologna Division was already retreating westward, hounded by British armored cars. In the afternoon, Montgomery's tanks surrounded and destroyed the remnants of the Ariete Division, whose tank crews mounted a gallant last stand in their "rolling coffins." Allied tanks and infantry now fanned out through a twelve-mile-wide hole in the Axis lines and threatened to envelop the remaining troops. "So now it had come," Rommel wrote, "the thing we had done everything in our power to avoid—our front broken and the fully motorized enemy streaming into our rear. Superior orders could no longer count. We had to save what there was to be saved."

Kesselring appeared at Rommel's headquarters and authorized him to

Taken prisoner by the British, the Afrikakorps commander, Wilhelm Ritter von Thoma *(left)*, describes his ordeal to General Montgomery *(right)*. Thoma had denounced Hitler's win-or-die order as "unparalleled madness." Rather than retreat, however, he pinned on his medals and drove alone in a tank into the thick of the battle.

defy Hitler's victory-or-death command. Rommel gave the order to retreat at half past three that afternoon, and his surviving units immediately began inching down the traffic-choked coast road toward Fuka. The Italian infantry divisions in the southern sector, lacking vehicles and separated from the rest of the retreating force, were left to shift for themselves; most of them surrendered. Hitler and Mussolini's approval of the retreat reached Rommel late that afternoon, too late to save thousands of Axis soldiers who had been killed and captured in the intervening thirty-six hours. His total strength now stood at 22,000 men. Defeated and disillusioned, Rommel and the remnants of the proud Panzerarmee hurried west with the Allies at their heels, back through the battlegrounds where they had savored victories, back to Tripoli and the final reckoning beyond. ✚

Face buried in his hands, a soldier who surrendered to Allied forces near El Alamein slumps beside a fellow prisoner of war.

"The Dead Are the Lucky Ones"

"The whole horizon seemed to burn and shudder," wrote one of Rommel's junior officers. Flames from exploding ammunition and blazing tanks flared against the sky. The sands west of El Alamein were littered with broken men and equipment—the sad, spectacular detritus of war and retreat. Time and again, the Afrikakorps had brought off miracles of bold attack. Now it would nearly perish defending itself against an opponent that had more tanks, planes, ammunition, and fuel, as well as men.

By November 2, 1942, the British had penetrated four miles into Rommel's front. Anticipating a breakthrough that could demolish his army, he ordered a withdrawal. Then came a command from the Führer: Stand fast; the Afrikakorps must follow "no other road than that to victory or death." That night, Rommel lay sleepless, "racking my brain for a way out of this plight for my poor troops." The dead are lucky, he concluded. "For them, it's all over."

Rommel agonized for a day, then ordered the retreat to resume. By then, more than 30,000 Axis troops had been killed or captured, many tanks and guns lost. As it was, infantry without motorized transport had to be left behind while truck convoys and the few remaining tanks set out along the coast road. Behind them, the remnants of the 90th Light Division fought a hit-and-run rearguard action. To slow the British pursuit, German sappers sowed the desert with mines and scrap metal (to fool the mine detectors). In deserted buildings, they left booby traps that exploded when toilets were flushed or crooked pictures straightened.

Four times British tank forces tried to cut the Germans off, but each thrust came too late. Then, on November 6, a drenching rain began, reducing the sandy roads to mush and bogging down the chase. With nature's help, Rommel saved his army from total rout. Over the weeks that followed, some 7,500 men, the remainder of his command, ran, fought, then ran again, all the way to the Libyan village of El Agheila, their starting point twenty months earlier. Ahead of them, a new threat loomed: An Anglo-American army had just come ashore in Algeria and Morocco.

In fading light, British troops *(above)* supported by an armored car harry retreating Germans and Italians west of El Alamein.

Streaming into Libya, a serpentine column of American trucks rolls westward on the coast road. The trucks and the cargoes they carried had reached Egypt via the Suez Canal as a part of the Lend-Lease program.

German infantrymen, one pushing his things in a homemade cart, trudge westward from El Alamein. Rommel wrote, "The army was no longer in a position to offer effective opposition to the British advance at any point."

Retreating German soldiers (left) carefully carry a wounded comrade on a litter. Long exposure to hardship and danger instilled a deep loyalty to one another in the men of the Afrikakorps.

On the heels of the Germans, trucks of the British Eighth Army move in single file to reduce the chance of hitting land mines.

A British mine-detecting team clears a path through a German minefield. Behind the sappers is a burned-out Matilda.

In Rommel's wake, the desert is strewn with discarded gear: blankets, bullets, grenades, sun helmets, papers, and food.

In a symbolic photograph distributed by the British after their victory at El Alamein, a Tommy with bayonet fixed stands guard

over an officer of the Afrikakorps, one of 10,000 Germans and 20,000 Italians taken prisoner in the pivotal battle of the desert war.

Acknowledgments

The editors thank the following individuals and institutions for their help in the preparation of this book: England: London—Christopher Hunt, Paul Kemp, Michael Willis, the Imperial War Museum. Wareham—George Forty, the Tank Museum. Federal Republic of Germany: Berlin—Heidi Klein, Bildarchiv Preussischer Kulturbesitz; Gabrielle Kohler, Archiv für Kunst und Geschichte; Wolfgang Streubel, Ullstein Bilderdienst. Dortmund—Franz Kurowski. Hamburg—Ilse Schmidt-Carell, Paul Schmidt-Carell. Koblenz—Meinrad Nilges, Bundesarchiv. Nuremberg—Hans-Rudolf Marseille. Rösrath-Hoffnungsthal—Helga Müller, Archiv J. K. Piekalkiewicz. German Democratic Republic: Berlin—Hannes Quaschinsky, ADN-Zentralbild. Italy: Milan—Camillo Albertini, Giancarlo Costa. Rome—Leonardo Andreoli; Marcello Marocchi, Istituto Luce S.p.A. United States of America: District of Columbia—Elizabeth Hill, National Archives; Eveline Nave, Library of Congress; George Snowden, Snowden Associates. Kentucky—John Purdy, Patton Museum of Cavalry and Armor. New Jersey—Al Collett. Virginia—George A. Petersen.

Picture Credits

Credits from left to right are separated by semicolons, from top to bottom by dashes. Cover: Presse-Seeger, Ebingen. 4, 5: National Archives, no. 131-21-18. 6: AP/Wide World Photos. 8, 9: Map by R. R. Donnelley and Sons Company, Cartographic Services. 10: Crown copyright, courtesy the Trustees of the Imperial War Museum, London. 12: AP/Wide World Photos. 13: Ullstein Bilderdienst, West Berlin. 14, 15: UPI/Bettmann Newsphotos. 17: Crown copyright, courtesy the Trustees of the Imperial War Museum, London. 18: Franz Kurowski, Dortmund. 20: Bundesarchiv, Koblenz. 21: Archiv J. K. Piekalkiewicz, Rösrath-Hoffnungsthal. 22, 23: Courtesy John Keener and George A. Petersen, photographed by Larry Sherer. 24: Archiv J. K. Piekalkiewicz, Rösrath-Hoffnungsthal. 26: Map by R. R. Donnelley and Sons Company, Cartographic Services. 29: Popperfoto, London. 33: Süddeutscher Verlag Bilderdienst, Munich. 34, 35: Ullstein Bilderdienst, West Berlin, inset map by R. R. Donnelley and Sons Company, Cartographic Services. 38: Keystone, Hamburg. 40, 41: Archiv J. K. Piekalkiewicz, Rösrath-Hoffnungsthal. 42, 43: National Archives, no. 242-EA-DC-6-251, inset, courtesy George A. Petersen from *Signal*, May 2, 1941, © Deutscher Verlag. 44, 45: From *Rommel: Battles and Campaigns* by Kenneth Macksey, Lionel Leventhal, Ltd., London, 1979—Photoreporters. 46, 47: Süddeutscher Verlag Bilderdienst, Munich; Ullstein Bilderdienst, West Berlin. 48, 49: Courtesy Time Inc. Picture Collection; FPG, New York. 50: Archiv J. K. Piekalkiewicz, Rösrath-Hoffnungsthal. 52, 53: UPI/Bettmann Newsphotos. 55: Map by R. R. Donnelley and Sons Company, Cartographic Services. 57: Süddeutscher Verlag Bilderdienst, Munich. 58: National Archives, no. 242-EAPC-6-M26—Bundesarchiv, Koblenz. 59: Süddeutscher Verlag Bilderdienst, Munich—courtesy Patton Museum of Cavalry and Armor, Ft. Knox, Kentucky, photographed by Mary S. Rezny.

61: AP/Wide World Photos. 62, 63: Bundesarchiv, Koblenz—Ullstein Bilderdienst, West Berlin. 66, 67: Bundesarchiv, Koblenz; Brigadier P. A. L. Vaux, Fleet, Hampshire. 68: Map by R. R. Donnelley and Sons Company, Cartographic Services. 71: Archiv J. K. Piekalkiewicz, Rösrath-Hoffnungsthal. 72, 73: From *Die Wüstenfüchse: Mit Rommel in Afrika* by Paul Carell, Bibliothek der Zeitgeschichte, West Berlin, 1989. 75: Map by R. R. Donnelley and Sons Company, Cartographic Services. 77: UPI/Bettmann Newsphotos. 79: Map by R. R. Donnelley and Sons Company, Cartographic Services. 80, 81: Bundesarchiv, Koblenz. 82, 83: Brigadier P. A. L. Vaux, Fleet, Hampshire. 84, 85: UPI/Bettmann Newsphotos. 86, 87: Courtesy George A. Petersen, photographed by Larry Sherer; Photoreporters. 88, 89: Art by John Batchelor; Robert Hunt Library, London. 90: Bundesarchiv, Koblenz—art by William Hennessy, Jr. 91: Bundesarchiv, Koblenz (2). 92, 93: AP/Wide World Photos—Süddeutscher Verlag Bilderdienst, Munich. 94: Bundesarchiv, Koblenz. 96: Franz Kurowski, Dortmund. 98: Bundesarchiv, Koblenz. 100, 101: Map by R. R. Donnelley and Sons Company, Cartographic Services. 102, 103: Archiv J. K. Piekalkiewicz, Rösrath-Hoffnungsthal—Süddeutscher Verlag Bilderdienst, Munich. 104, 105: Bundesarchiv, Koblenz. 106: UPI/Bettmann Newsphotos. 107: Camera Press, London (2). 109: Farabola, Milan. 110, 111: Bundesarchiv, Koblenz. 113: Map by R. R. Donnelley and Sons Company, Cartographic Services. 115: Bundesarchiv, Koblenz. 118, 119: Edimedia, Paris. 121: Map by R. R. Donnelley and Sons, Cartographic Services. 123: Süddeutscher Verlag Bilderdienst, Munich. 124, 125: ADN-Zentralbild, Berlin, DDR; Crown copyright, courtesy the Trustees of the Imperial War Museum, London. 126, 127: Bundesarchiv, Koblenz. 129: Bundesarchiv, Koblenz, fabric background, Paul Kennedy. 130, 131: Bundesarchiv, Koblenz, except top left, Lt. Col. George Forty (ret.). 132, 133: Süddeutscher Verlag Bilderdienst, Munich; Ullstein Bilderdienst, West Berlin—Crown copyright, courtesy the Trustees of the Imperial War Museum, London. 134, 135: From *Mit Rommel in der Wüste* by Volkmar Kühn, Motorbuch Verlag, Stuttgart, 1987. 136-138: Süddeutscher Verlag Bilderdienst, Munich. 139: From *Rommel* by Silvio Bertoldi, Istituto Geografico de Agostini-Novara. 140, 141: Farabola, Milan. 142: Süddeutscher Verlag Bilderdienst, Munich. 143: Map by R. R. Donnelley and Sons Company, Cartographic Services. 145: British Official Newsreel from Pathé News. 146-149: UPI/Bettmann Newsphotos. 151: Crown copyright, courtesy the Trustees of the Imperial War Museum, London. 153: Courtesy George A. Petersen, from *Signal*, no. 22, November 1942. 154, 155: Courtesy George A. Petersen, from *Signal*, no. 22, November 1942, except bottom right, Süddeutscher Verlag Bilderdienst, Munich. 159: Map by R. R. Donnelley and Sons Company, Cartographic Services. 160: Bildarchiv Preussischer Kulturbesitz, West Berlin. 161-166: Bundesarchiv, Koblenz. 167: Stato Maggiore Aeronautica, Rome—Bundesarchiv, Koblenz. 168, 169: Bundesarchiv, Koblenz. 171: British Official Newsreel from Pathé News. 173: Map by R. R. Donnelley and Sons Company, Cartographic Services. 175: Süddeutscher Verlag Bilderdienst, Munich. 176, 177: Crown copyright, courtesy the Trustees of the Imperial War Museum, London. 178, 179: Crown copyright, courtesy the Trustees of the Imperial War Museum, London; Bob Landry for LIFE. 180, 181: Crown copyright, courtesy the Trustees of the Imperial War Museum, London—Camera Press, London. 182: Bob Landry for LIFE—Crown copyright, courtesy the Trustees of the Imperial War Museum, London. 183: Bob Landry for LIFE. 184, 185: AP/Wide World Photos.

Bibliography

Agar-Hamilton, J. A. I., and L. C. F. Turner, eds., *The Sidi Rezeg Battles, 1941.* Cape Town, South Africa: Oxford University Press, 1957.

Ansel, Walter, *Hitler and the Middle Sea.* Durham, N.C.: Duke University Press, 1972.

"Autowerkstatt—ein Quadratkilometer gross." *Signal*, November 2, 1942.

Bekker, Cajus, *The Luftwaffe War Diaries.* Transl. and ed. by Frank Ziegler. Garden City, N.Y.: Doubleday, 1968.

Bender, Roger James, and Richard D. Law, *Uniforms, Organization and History of the Afrikakorps.* San Jose, Calif.: R. James Bender, 1973.

Bergot, Erwan, *The Afrika Korps.* New York: Charter Books, 1975.

Bingham, J. K. W., and Werner Haupt, *North African Campaign, 1940-1943.* London: Macdonald, 1969.

Carell, Paul, *The Foxes of the Desert.* Transl. by Mervyn Savill. Toronto: Bantam Books, 1962.

Carver, Michael, *Dilemmas of the Desert War: A New Look at the Libyan Campaign, 1940-1942.* Bloomington: Indiana University Press, 1986.

Department of Military Art and Engineering, *The War in North Africa.* Part 1. West Point, N.Y.: United States Military Academy, 1944.

Douglas-Home, Charles, *Rommel.* New York: Saturday Review Press, 1973.

Ellis, William S., "Malta: The Passion of Freedom." *National Geographic*, June 1989.

Forty, George, *The Road to Alexandria.* Vol. 1 of *Afrika Korps at War.* London: Ian Allan, 1978.

Gibson, Hugh, ed., *The Ciano Diaries.* Garden City, N.Y.: Doubleday, 1973.

Held, Werner, *Fighter! Luftwaffe Fighter Planes and Pilots.* Englewood Cliffs, N.J.: Prentice-Hall, 1979.

Hogg, Ian V., *German Artillery of World War Two.* London: Arms and Armour Press, 1975.

Holmes, Richard, *Bir Hacheim: Desert Citadel.* New York: Ballantine Books, 1971.

Irving, David, *Trail of the Fox.* London: Weidenfeld and Nicolson, 1977.

Jackson, W. G. F., *The Battle for North Africa, 1940-43.* New York: Mason/Charter, 1975.

Kesselring, Albert, *Kesselring: A Soldier's Record.* Westport, Conn.: Greenwood Press, 1970.

Kurowski, Franz, *Der Afrikafeldzug: Rommels Wüstenkrieg, 1941-1943 (The Panzers Are Rolling in Africa: With Rommel in the Desert War, 1941-1943).* Leoni, W.Ger.: Druffel Verlag, 1986.

Law, Richard D., and Craig W. H. Luther, *Rommel: A Narrative and Pictorial History.* San Jose, Calif.: R. James Bender, 1980.

Lewin, Ronald:
The Life and Death of the Afrika Korps. New York: Quadrangle, 1977.
Rommel as Military Commander. London: B. T. Batsford, 1968.

Liddell Hart, B. H., ed., *The Rommel Papers.* Transl. by Paul Findlay. New York: Da Capo Press, 1982.

Lucas, James, *Panzer Army Africa.* London: Macdonald and Jane's, 1977.

The Luftwaffe, by the Editors of Time-Life Books (The Epic of Flight series). Alexandria, Va.: Time-Life Books, 1982.

Macksey, Kenneth:
Afrika Korps. New York: Ballantine Books, 1968.
Rommel: Battles and Campaigns. New York: Mayflower Books, 1979.

Mellenthin, F. W. von, *Panzer Battles: A Study of the Emplacement of Armor in the Second World War.* Transl. by H. Betzler, ed. by L. C. F. Turner. New York: Ballantine Books, 1971.

Müller, Werner, *Die 8,8 cm Flak 18-36-37-41.* Dorheim, W.Ger.: Podzun-Pallas-Verlag, 1986.

Playfair, I. S. O., et al., *The Mediterranean and Middle East:*
Vol. 2, *"The Germans Come to the Help of Their Ally" (1941).* London: Her Majesty's Stationery Office, 1956.
Vol. 3, *British Fortunes Reach Their Lowest Ebb.* London: Her Majesty's Stationery Office, 1960.
Vol. 4, *The Destruction of the Axis Forces in Africa.* London: Her Majesty's Stationery Office, 1966.

Rutherford, Ward, *The Biography of Field Marshal Erwin Rommel.* London: Hamlyn, 1981.

Schmidt, Heinz Werner, *With Rommel in the Desert.* London: George G. Harrap, 1951.

Shores, Christopher, *Duel for the Sky.* Garden City, N.Y.: Doubleday, 1985.

Shores, Christopher, and Hans Ring, *Fighters over the Desert: The Air Battles in the Western Desert, June 1940 to December 1942.* London: Neville Spearman, 1969.

Toliver, Raymond F., and Trevor J. Constable, *Fighter Aces of the Luftwaffe.* Fallbrook, Calif.: Aero, 1977.

Young, Desmond, *Rommel: The Desert Fox.* New York: Quill, 1978.

Index

Numerals in italics indicate an illustration of the subject mentioned.

Rezegh, 78; on Battle of El Alamein, 144, 145; on British retreat, 99; on defense of Bir Hacheim, 122; on Gazala, 105; on Montgomery's failure to counterattack at El Alamein, 157-158; on Rommel, 47, 105; as Rommel's intelligence chief, 71, 99; as Rommel's operations chief, 122, 149; on supply shortages, 149

Mersa Brega: 25-27, 84

Mersa Matruh: 11-13, 138-140, 142

Messervy, Frank: captured and escapes, 111, 123; commands 4th Armored Brigade, 57; commands Indian 4th Division, 54; commands 7th Armored Division, 111; and defense of Knightsbridge box, 123

Montgomery, Bernard: commands Eighth Army, 150, *151*, 156, 160; constructs diversionary dummy water pipeline, 164, 169; fails to counterattack at El Alamein, 157-158; prepares all-out assault on Panzerarmee Afrika, 171, *map 173*

Moorehead, Alan: 140

Morshead, Leslie James: commands Australian troops at Tobruk, 35

Mussolini, Benito: 84, 170; authorizes Rommel to attack Benghazi, 100; flies to North Africa, *140-141*; Hitler on, 19; interest in North Africa, 8-10; leaves North Africa, 148; meets with Hitler, 11, *12*, 104; meets with Rommel, 158; orders invasion of Egypt, 10; puts Italian forces under Rommel's command, 76; replaces Graziani, 64

N

Neame, Philip: captured, 31; commands British and Commonwealth forces in Libya, 31

Nehring, Walther: commands Afrikakorps, 114, 156; wounded, 156

Neumann-Silkow, Walther: commands 15th Panzer Division, *67*; commands Libyan frontier defenses, 52

Norrie, C. W. M.: commands XXX Corps, 69, 73, 78

North Africa: *map 8-9;* fighting conditions in, 7-8, 38-39, 56, 129; heavy rains in, 70, *71;* Hitler's lack of interest in, 8; Italian army defeated in, 7-8; Libya's strategic value in, 9-10, 18; Luftwaffe camouflage in, *96;* Mussolini's interest in, 8-10; OKW and Italian collapse in, 17; Rommel on conditions in, 7, 28; use of radios in, 58; Wavell as British commander in, 26; Wehrmacht operations in (Operation Sunflower), 18

O

O'Connor, Richard: as British commander in Egypt, 13, 15-16, 31; captured, 31

Olbrich, Herbert: commands 5th Panzer Regiment, 28, 32, 36-37; dismissed from command, 37

Operation Barbarossa: *See* Eastern front; Soviet Union

Operation Battleaxe: *See* British and Commonwealth forces

Operation Brevity: *See* British and Commonwealth forces

Operation Crusader: *See* British and Commonwealth forces

Operation Sunflower: *See* North Africa

Operation Supercharge: *See* Panzerarmee Afrika

Operation Venezia: *See* Gazala, Battle of; Tobruk, Battle of

P

Palestine: British residents in Egypt flee to, 140

Panzerarmee Afrika: all-out assault on at El Alamein (Operation Supercharge), 171-174, *map 173,* 177; campaign plan for, 137; deployment at El Alamein, 142, 152-156, 158; established, 97; and food shortages, 161; invades Egypt, 137-142; losses at El Alamein, 150, 157, 174-175, *176,* 177, *184-185;* reinforced and resupplied at El Alamein, 144, 147, 151-152; retreats to El Agheila, 177, *180-181, 183;* retreats to Fuka, 174-175; Rommel commands, 97, 116, 142; withdraws from El Alamein, 157, 159, 173-174. *See also* Afrikakorps; Panzergruppe Afrika

Panzergruppe Afrika: 71, 76, 80; created, 64; size of, 66. *See also* Afrikakorps; Panzerarmee Afrika

Paulewiecz, Lieutenant: at Gazala, 114-115

Paulus, Friedrich von: on inspection trip to Tobruk, 39-40; as OKW deputy chief, 39

Point 206 (Libyan frontier): 52, 54, 56

Ponath, Gustav: in assault on Tobruk, 36-37; commands 8th Machine-Gun Battalion, 24, 28, 31, 36; killed, 37

Prittwitz, Heinrich von: commands 15th Panzer Division, 32; killed, 32

Q

Qattara Depression: *142,* 156

R

Radios: use in North Africa, 58

Raeder, Erich: urges occupation of Malta, 101-102

Ramsden, W. H.: commands 50th Division, 125-126

Ravenstein, Johann von: captured, 82; commands 5th Light Division, 52, 72; commands 21st Panzer Division, 82

Reissmann, Werner: commands 104th Infantry Regiment (3d Battalion), 118

Ringler, Ralf: 133, 172

Ritchie, Neil: attempts to recapture the Cauldron, 118-120; commands Eighth Army, 81, 104; and defense of Gazala, 105,

111, 123, 125, 127; poor tactics at Gazala, 111, 118

Rommel, Erwin: *42-47, 104-105;* on Afrikakorps's retreat, 181; asks for and is denied relief of command, 152; assaults Egyptian frontier, *map 79,* 80-81; assaults Hill 209, 39-40; attacks at Bir el Gubi, 83-84; Auchinleck on, 42; awarded Knight's Cross with Oak Leaves and Swords, 25, 97; background of, 18-19; on battle at Mersa Matruh, 140; on Battle of El Alamein, 144, 148, 158, 170; on Battle of Gazala, 110; British commando attack on, 70; on British tactics at Gazala, 111; captures Tobruk, 106, 128, 137; changes tactics at Gazala, 117; character of, 30, 42, 105-106; chosen to command Afrikakorps, 18-19; Churchill on, 42, 52, 61, 105; on collapse of Italian army, 19; on command, 47; command style, 54, 65, 116-117; commands Panzerarmee Afrika, 97, 116, 142; commands Panzergruppe Afrika, 64; commands 7th Panzer Division, 19, 86; complains of Italian inefficiency, 151; on conditions in North Africa, 7, 28; confers with Kesselring and Cavallero, 98, 152; confrontation with Gariboldi, 27-28; confrontation with Kesselring and Bastico, 137; confrontation with Streich, 30, 32; counterattacks at Sidi Rezegh, *map 75;* creates propaganda victory, 62-64; on desert tactics, 86; engages in air reconnaissance, 21, 29, 44; enters the Cauldron, 118; fails to anticipate British attack, 66-67, 69-71; feints toward Mechili, 100; fired on by Italian riflemen, 30; flanks Gazala Line, 110-116; fortifies Bardia, 66; fortifies Halfaya Pass, 51, *52-53,* 66; fortifies Sollum, 51; on fuel shortages, 152; and Goebbels, 160; Goebbels on, 42; goes on defensive at El Alamein, 158; and Göring, 160; Halder's opinion of, 39; Hitler upgrades his command, 97; ill health, 152, 157, 158-160; influence on Hitler, 137; inspects Afrikakorps, *6;* Kesselring on, 158; map of Tobruk, *59;* meets with Hitler, 158-160; meets with Mussolini, 158; Mellenthin on, 47, 105; misunderstands British offensive, 73; OKW rebukes, 28; opinion of Italian army, 12-13, 37, 51-52, 61; out of touch with his operations staff, 81; at party rally, *162-163;* personal contact with his men, 40, 44, *46-47;* plans to pursue British Eighth Army, 137; prepares to assault Tobruk, 65-67; prepares for Battle of Tobruk, 122; prepares to recapture Tobruk, 101, 104; presence at the front, 40, *44-46;* promoted, 100; promoted to field marshal, 128, 137; as propaganda figure, *42-43;* rebukes Wolz, 114; recuperates in Germany, 100-101, 158-160; relations with Bastico, 64-65, 66; returns to El Alamein, 169; on